Sprookje

Anthony van Leeuwen

Paperback ISBN: 979-8-3589692-9-2
Hardback ISBN: 979-8-9871521-1-9

Cover art by Patrick Moran
Book design and back cover by Lauren Grosskopf

Special Thanks

KEVIN SESSUMS
MICHAEL GRAVES
SARAH METCALF
DIANA BLUE
BESSEL VAN DER KOLK
STEFANIE AUGUST
LAUREN GROSSKOPF
PATRICK MORAN
AMP & LORENZO

Thank you to the cafes of New York City
Where so much of this piece was created
And that gave me a "home" to do so

Sprookje was birthed in Lollino's
I remained—fairly—monogamous to them for three years
Perhaps there was the occasional indiscretion

But since they closed their doors
I embraced a poly-amorous viewpoint with my cafes:

Café Flor
787 Coffee (East Village and Chelsea)
Murphy's Door
Café Aronne
Sogano Toscano

And to all the friendly baristas
Who made my coffee and were part of my day,
This project, and my memories of creating it.

Sprookje

(DUTCH: FAIRY TALE)

Dedicated to
MICHAEL CANTOR

"Some day you will be old enough
To start reading fairy tales again."

—C.S. Lewis

Once upon a time
There was a boy
And there was a boy

Forbidden love
Are they supposed to be together?

Part I

Two men are walking toward each other
Along 19th St. in Chelsea, Manhattan
On a beautiful mid-afternoon summer day

It is the 16th of September, 2020

One is wearing a green hoodie...
As they approach their eyes meet

And feelings of familiarity take place in each
They slow down

The man in the green hoodie pauses before him
And begins to speak...

"Excuse me,
Are you Dutch?

Where are you from?

I feel we have met many years ago
...Twenty years ago
Were you living in Amsterdam
In December 2000?

I was living in Leiden

Did you ever go out
And experience the nightlife
That winter?

To Warmosesstraat?

To Club Cockring?

In the darkroom at Cockring?

Did you ever meet a boy
In the dark
Who told you his name was Michael
And he was a student in London?

That is me!

It is you!
It is really you!
I have dreamed of this moment
For seventeen years..."

Yes!
It was incredibly special and magical
It is still magical
You have remained in my life
In the most enchanting
Unimaginable ways
Through dreams and inspiration
At the most poignant times in my life
I have searched for you
Wanting you to know
That *you* have provided
The *greatest* source of wonderment
In my life

*

I'm so sorry I kissed you
And walked away
All those years ago
When we saw each other
For the *first* time in the light
After *all* of our nights in the dark
I was not out
I was not comfortable being myself
My name is not even Michael
It's Anthony
I'm sorry I told you Michael
I wasn't ready to be Anthony
Doing all the *things* we did
That was Michael

I had just begun
To come out of a dark period
When we met
I was about to enter another–
My struggle with being gay
But when I arrived in the Netherlands
I was in a liminal space

Between the two dark ones
A place of light
And magic
A happier place
Certainly happier
Than the previous three years

It was only a few weeks
Before meeting you
That I began to *choose* life again
My brother died in a car accident
Three years before we met
As I waded through grief
My sexuality became harder
To push down
I didn't want to be gay
I was envious of Joe
I wished
Death had come for me
Not him

When I went to London
Part of me hoped
I could disappear
Into the clubs and drugs
And slip away
Completely
To the other side

*

But!
I was doing ecstasy
And the DJ's and club scene
In London at that time
Were on fire!
So that wasn't likely to happen
In fact

It was making me happier
And I was attracting
Other *happy* people
Who knew I was ahead of science
And the use of 'e' for trauma
They do that now
Perhaps not the same doses
I was doing
But it served a purpose
Brought me to a place
Where I understood
It was okay to go on…
And be happy

*

It was a time to *celebrate*
And I had my *best* friend—
Mike
Waiting for me in…
Amsterdam!
He was visiting his brother
Who was studying in Leiden

Mike was the *perfect* person to meet
At the beginning stages
Of emerging out of the dark from Joe
He was the person
From the first full day without Joe
That was in the trenches with me
A bomb destroyed my world
He was the soldier by my side
As I entered a war with grief

We were living in the fraternity house
I could wake him at any hour
To talk
Or cry

He was there
I was *so* happy to see Mike
And tell him first and foremost
How much better I felt
He was a brother
In head and heart
Like the relationship I believe
Would have grown with Joe
Had it not been for Mike's friendship
And the unconventional direction
My life took after university
I wouldn't have been in Leiden
I wouldn't have met…
You

*

Oh how I felt a *surge*
A real love for life again
It was *so* bright
In my heart and head
Excitement for life
Poured through me
Except for the life of a gay man

But I had almost a month
In the Netherlands
To give myself
Or rather… Michael
An experience
Before I left *him* in Europe

I felt safe exploring my sexuality
In Amsterdam
Nobody knew where I was
Or what I was doing
It was such
Private

Precious
Sacred time with myself
Freedom to *explore*
Loving myself enough—
At least for those few weeks—
To give my heart
What it desired
Before the cage of my mind
Conditioned to live the "correct" way
Imprisoned Michael
In Amsterdam
He was free to live
His way

*

Oh it was an *amazing* time
To be in Amsterdam!
I'm sure you recall
The Gay Capitol of Europe at the time
It felt electric!
Alive!
But I was just a wallflower
In this New World
I couldn't talk to people

The best wallflower spot I had
Was at Havana's
You remember Havana's?
They had that little narrow balcony
With a couple tables and chairs
That overlooked the dance floor
And the circular bar

I would sit in the corner
Always a corner
Observing all the gay men below
Amazed and envious

How they interacted with one another
Dancing, mingling, and laughing!

*

One night
A lone man walked in
He had a blue knit cap on
With dirty-blond hair
Peeking from underneath
And a coat that looked
Slightly big on him
He stood in the center
With a slight smile on his face
Simply taking in the moment
He felt peaceful
Present

'If there is *anyone*
I wish to know—
It is him,' I thought.

But that would mean uprooting myself
And *actually* going to talk to him
I was too shy for that
And eventually he left
That was a typical night
I was in the room
But all the action was in my head
In the light of the bars
Until
The clocks in the village
Struck midnight
And I'd make my way
Toward the cobblestones
Of Warmoesstraat
Into Cockring
Into the darkroom

Where I met
You

*

Yes, I remember the sex we had
It was hot, and erotic, no doubt!
But as the nights went on
We found one another
In the dark
Without ever seeing the other's face
Sensing
Knowing
It was the same boy
From the night before
And the night before that
Simply by our vibrations
And intimacy began to burrow

Oh I can still see your silhouette
With the tiny bit of light
Near the staircase
Quickly maneuvering
Through the men
Between us
To get to me
It was so sexy
The urgency with which you moved
Once you sensed me
Standing
Waiting
And in an instant
You were in front of me
Filling me with excitement
That we we were able to continue
From the night before

I wanted so badly

To simply touch a man
To caress him
To hold him
It felt so freeing
When you allowed me
To explore you
You were so gentle
It felt so peaceful
And grounding
In your arms

I can still feel my hand
As I placed it on your heart
I wanted to feel it beating
Wiping the sweat from your brow
Running my fingers through your hair
I wanted to feel all of you
Hugging you closer to me
Feeling your breath on me
Exhaling against you
As we breathed in unison

*

The last night we were together
When we spoke for the first time
I was so nervous to speak to you—
Someone I was so intimate with—
The depth of intimacy we shared
Was more than I'd ever experienced
As if we were floating
Through empty space
Far from the darkroom
Far from Earth
Far from our three-dimensional forms
We were simply energy

*

All I could do was answer
Your simple questions
Never thinking to ask you the same
Not even your name

*

Then you asked,
"Do you know what this is?"

It made me *so* nervous
I didn't understand what you meant
And did not know what to say
My brain could barely form sentences

So there was a moment of silence
Before you answered your own question
So confidently
So *certain*

"This is love," you said.

*

I didn't know what to say
Still trapped in the belief
Love
Was not allowed
Between two men

*

I grew up in a time and place
In the Midwest
Where it was not even around me
To know *this* existed
How do you be something
You don't know exists?

And when I did know
It was something to be laughed at
Or more accurately...feared
Have your guard up
Around *"those"* people

When the plague struck
The religious preacher's
Now had proof!
Being gay was a *huge* sin
And God's punishment for it
Was a gay cancer
That was *killing* them
Well, *all* that
Had this 9-year-old Catholic boy
Running deeper into the closet
He didn't realize he was in

That was my spot
On the gay history timeline
My environment
For the development of this homo

*

When you asked me
If I had a place we could go
I did
But said no
I'm sorry
I was too afraid having you there
Would marry the lives
Of Anthony and Michael
I wasn't ready for that
I *did* want
To spend more time with you
Ohhhh, how I did!
I was disappointed

9

When you said you had guests
Then you buttoned up quickly
And left the darkroom
In one fluid moment
I felt rejected
Never realizing
I had always left first
And how that must have felt

But like Cinderella
And the clock striking midnight
I *had* to leave
Straight out the door
To the station
I would rush to get in bed
Before the sun rose
Where the night would be
A dream
You
A dream

*

I felt insecure when you left
I waited in the darkroom
A little bit longer
To give you time to disappear
In the crowded club
But when I pushed open the door
You were there, squatting down
With your arms resting on your knees
Hands clasped, looking up at *me*
Your smile was *beaming*
Your eyes *shining* love
To *me?*

But being in the dark
Living in the darkness

The light was so bright
Not from the club
But from *you*
Ohhhh my heart melts now
At the recollection of that moment
The image is burned in my heart
You hadn't rejected me
You wanted to be *ready*
To catch me
Before *I* dashed off
To be ready
To look into my eyes
For the *first* time
After all of our nights in the dark

Your love *stunned* me
Speechless
I had *zero* self-love as a gay man
And RuPaul speaks the truth
If you can't love yourself
How the *hell*
You gonna love somebody else?

You looked so beautiful
I didn't expect you to be there
I lied about my name
Frazzled
What was I to do?
Continue the lie?
But you were so sweet
How could I do that?
How could I tell the truth
And be hated by you
I already hated myself
So I bent down
Kissed you
And ran away
Not from you and your love

But from coming out to myself

*

I can still feel the moment
As I approached your lips
Still feel them
Right before they touched
I *wanted* to see your eyes
Up close
But could only look half up
I was afraid you'd see
How broken I was
I had no idea how to receive your love
I *did* see your eyes
And the love went through me
Burrowed inside
And waited

*

When I saw you
I *instantly* knew
You were the *same* man
I saw in Havana's
The man I wished upon
With your blue knit cap on

We did get to know each other
Perhaps not in the conventional way
But in a deeper, otherworldly way

*

I did go back to the darkroom
The following night
You were not there
Or, if you were
Not at the same time as I

Regardless, I did not stay
I was disappointed
And concerned
That my actions hurt you
Something felt empty
Even with a darkroom full of men

*

The next day I returned to London
Then America a few days later
But after nine months
In the conservative Midwest
The closeted faggot in me
Had to get out

My friend Gregg from university
Presented an opportunity
To move out west
So I went
I decided on a gay life in California
And a straight one in Michigan

9/11 was the day I was to fly
My family encouraged me
To scratch my move
Stay "home"
That was *never* an option for me
I had to get out
I knew my life
Was *not* there

I flew three days later
And found myself living
In an idyllic beach paradise
Far from the Midwest suburb
A little place
Called Laguna Beach

Oh, it's gorgeous!
The beaches
Are some of the *most* beautiful
I've ever seen in the world
The ocean
With Catalina Island in the distance
Exquisite sunsets full of color
And the quaint town center
It was a perfect bubble to heal in
After Joe and London

I became a barista
At the Koffee Klatch
In the tiny gayborhood
I found an old storybook bungalow
Nestled in the hills for a home
It overlooked the ocean
And had trees all around
It felt like I was living
In a pink birdhouse
Yes!
It was pink!
Bright Pepto-Bismol pink
Although faded over the years
I had a little balcony
Looking out to the ocean
It was so tranquil
A gentle haven to lay my head
In preparation to come out

*

And two years after we met
I did
Mike was the first person
I chose to bridge
The dual lives
The funny thing is

Mike picked the same night to ask
We were really in tune in that way
But both still nervous
And avoided the subject the whole night
Until after the bars closed
And we were back at Mike's apartment
Smoking pot, laughing, being silly
Finally around 3:00 a.m.
He knocked on the closet door
And came in
His words were *sooo*
Lovingly
Chosen and expressed
With *such* emotional maturity
For someone of twenty-five

"Look, Anthony
I want to ask you something
And before I do
I want you to know
That it doesn't matter to me
What your answer is
Really
You're a great friend
And we've been through a lot together
And you're someone
I always want in my life."

"Likewise," I said.

"Great, then do you know
What I'm going to ask you?"

I nodded

"Well, are you?"

I nodded "yes" again

Even his next question
Such brotherly love instinct
The need to ask and *know*

"Are you ok?"

Ohhhh, what a shining star!

*

Mike was also
Unbeknownst to him
At the beginning of my Gay 101
In Amsterdam a few years prior
It was the first time
We traveled to Amsterdam together
I was backpacking around Europe
He was beginning his year
Of studying abroad in England
We stayed at the Globe Hostel
Near Centraal Station
Wandered to the Red Light District
And into the private video booths
Where, for the first time
My eyes saw
Gay!
Sex!
I can still hear Mike
Coming down the hall of booths
Trying to find me

"Anthony! Where are you?
You done?
Let's go to a coffeeshop."

No, I wasn't done!
I *suppose*
I did lose track of time in there—

And *many* Guilders
What can I say?
I was mesmerized
My eyes had stars in them
Porn stars

*

Ohhhh, the night I came out to Mike
We had such a laugh afterward
When he connected the dots over the years
Of the dual lives
Mike was a good friend like that
The person that knew me better
Than I knew myself
Because he paid attention to my life
Cherished the times we spent together
And liked to reminisce

"You mean that 4th of July in Chicago
When I visited you
And you didn't come home
That was your *first* experience
With a guy?"

"Yes," I said.

"And *all* those times
We went to the Red Light District
Into the video booths
I'm assuming
It wasn't for the straight porn."

"No," I said.

"Ahhhh, it all makes more sense now
How funny!"

It was good to laugh with him
Like *that* again
Like I was back
And he had his friend back
All of him
After some war-like times

"You know I love you," he added
Before we went to sleep

"I know. I love you too."

*

The following spring in 2003
I felt happy
Now that *that* one moment was done
I had a blank canvas
To create my next chapter
At first it was daunting
I hadn't thought about life
After coming out
Because of Joe
My mortality was put
Right in my face
I honestly didn't think
I had long to live
He didn't
That's why I zipped around the world
To see all I could see
Then went to London hoping to die
Because I didn't want to be gay
But I was
And I was only twenty-six
What *was* I going to do with myself?

Cue: a Hollywood club
English friends were beginning a year

Of traveing around the world
While laughing and catching up
I shared the dreams I was considering
Since coming out

I wanted to live in the Netherlands
The collective consciousness
Was more accepting and tolerant
With less mental and emotional pollution
Toward gays than anywhere else
Having recently legalized
Gay marriage at the time
The first country to do so

My soul breathed easier there
Like stepping out of a smog filled city
Into Shangri-La

Of course I didn't understand it
Intellectually as that
I just knew I wanted to be *there*
I felt a better life could be lived there
Perhaps like my Dutch ancestors felt
Decades earlier immigrating to America
Now the tide had turned
And it was time to immigrate back

*

I had come to love the café culture
Working at the Koffee Klatch
So I dreamt of a café in Amsterdam
As well as traveling to Australia
Laguna was suppose to be a stopover
For a few months on my way to Oz
Before my issues grounded me

I shared these dreams with my friends

They invited me to Australia
At the end of the year
Then suggested we start a café
In England *together*
Well, they were so lovable
I said, "yes!" on the spot
It felt like I went to Hollywood
And my dreams came true
Except for the café being in Amsterdam
But now two people I loved
Were part of the dream

*

After they left
The self-love kept growing
From *deep* inside
Revealed itself completely
That stunning, pristine feeling
Awoken!

My sub-conscious knocked
'Hey!' it said.
'You know this feeling you're feeling?
This needle in a haystack feeling?
You've felt it before
Remember?'

'Oh my god!
The boy from Amsterdam!
He was right!
This *is* love.'

The same feeling inside me
Was *exactly* what I felt in your arms
Ohhhh, my heart sank
That I didn't know your name
Or how to find you

I sent you thoughts
Of love and gratitude
For coming into my life
From my pink birdhouse
Bittersweetly, as summer approached

But I made a promise to you
That whenever I thought of you
I would send you love
Wishes for happiness, health
And that life was being kind to you
It was all I could do
The least I could do
Considering I couldn't find you
For giving the most precious gift
That you felt love for me
And expressed it

*

Then
I had a dream of you
We were in Amsterdam
Walking down a cobblestone street
Holding hands
The image was of our backs
Walking away
You had a white T-shirt on
Your hair was shorter—
A buzz cut
It made me so happy to see you
Even if only in a dream

I also had visions of you
Your image would come floating by...
I was spending a lot of time
With Laguna's nature
I had moved out of the pink house

Down the hill
To the beach for the summer
Before leaving for Australia
It was a charming neighborhood
Tucked away with an intimate beach
Called Victoria
If you didn't know a local
Or weren't one
You probably wouldn't have found it
Back then anyway

*

Everyday I'd bike to the café for work
Do errands in the afternoon
And return down the little windy road
To snuggle in at the beach
It was my television
The sunsets, the different people
Playing and swimming
Sometimes dolphins or seals went by
It was a different show each night
And *so* peaceful
I felt you there most
It was *strong*
I wondered
Perhaps my thoughts of love *did* reach you
From the pink house
And were returned with these visions
Dreams
And feelings of you
Sometimes it felt *so* powerful
I second-guessed myself
And questioned if you were *actually*
Physically near me
It was so surreal
I was feeling you inside
and all around me

*

About a year prior to this time
I decided to take a break from men
I was building courage
And battling depression
To come out to my family
A friend gifted me a *beautiful*
Hard cover diary from 1974
With gold leaf and quotes
From Khalil Gibran
I tried to write down one positive
Experience or thought
To take from each day
Sometimes
I would be lost in worry or fear
And not write anything
For several days
But then forced myself to go back
Through each day and write *something*

I made it *The Love Diary*
Instinctively cultivating self-love
In preparing to come out
Before I consciously understood
That was what I was doing

I also romantically wondered
If on the last day of the diary
After a year of writing gratitude
True love would appear
A playful thought
That danced in my head
And was then let go

*

Then, one day

16

In July 2003
The 17th to be exact
And the last day of the diary
From the first entry
On the 18th of July 2002
I was on one of the free blue trolleys
That Laguna provided
Up and down the coast during summer
For the tourist season
My bike was in the shop
Due to an accident the day before
So I hopped on the trolley
To go to the gym
Otherwise, I wouldn't have been on it

About a mile from Victoria Beach
Near the Koffee Klatch
The trolley stopped
As it did
I noticed two girls and a boy
Walking down the street
The boy had blond buzz cut hair
A white T-shirt and khaki shorts
Orange framed sunglasses
With yellow lenses
But I could still see his eyes
Through the light lenses
I had blue sunglasses on
But transparent enough to also see my eyes
And our eyes did connect for a moment
I felt something…familiar

The trolley started to pull away
I found the man attractive
And turned to take a second look
Wondering if he was gay
Relying upon the second look
An innate way of protection

I think many gay men
Of certain generations relied upon
From staring too much
With the first look
For fear that they may not be gay
Or worse, homophobic
And attack verbally
Or worse, physically

When I looked
I saw all three of their backs
The man did not take a second look
But one of the girls did
And looked right at me
She smiled
So I smiled back
And as I looked at the man
His presence
His energy
Still felt…*so* familiar
It wasn't until the trolley
Was a couple blocks away
That the image of the girl I smiled at
Made me think she looked Dutch
And the dots connected immediately

'Oh my god!
That *can't* be…
Can it?'

When I stepped off the trolley
I turned for a moment
In the direction it had come
Wondering
Whether I should go back
And just see
But doubt and insecurity crept in
I thought that if it was you

Or if that man was gay
And attracted to me
He would have done a second look
Or
Perhaps you didn't remember me
'That would be too magical.'
The man
Who had been *so* much on my mind
And in my heart
For the past few months
After realizing
Our *beautiful* time together
That only happens in films

I didn't believe
That it *could* be you

*

My plan:
Work until the end of summer
Visit my family in autumn
Then head to Australia
Followed by England
But!
I couldn't get you out of my thoughts

My heart had an idea
Immediately
My head spoke up

'Mr. Heart,' my head said.
'We have worked together for many years
I have assisted where I could along the way
When you've wanted something
Some desires were trickier than others
But we figured it out...together
But!

As your head
I must duly note for the record
That *this!*
This is your wildest idea yet
I have computed the probability
Of this happening
Of you finding this man
Let's just say nothing is impossible
But this
This is nearly impossible
Do you really want to spend
Your precious time on Earth
Looking for a man
You don't know anything about
Not *even* his name
Or, if he is *even* from Amsterdam
The odds
Well
They are against you
I'm sorry my friend
I know it's not what you want to hear
Besides
You saw him so briefly in the light
How would you recognize him?'

When finished
My heart *confidently*
As *confidently* as you stated
'This is love.'
Replied

'Mr. Head, dear friend
We *have* worked well together
Over the years
Your opinion and advice
Are *always* welcome
Always respected
Your opinion on this matter is *duly* noted

For the record
I'm fully aware of the chances
Of finding this man
But!
I don't care
I have to try
Yes, he was all bundled up with his coat
And blue knit cap
But I did see his eyes
And his smile
If I can get a good look in his eyes
I *will* recognize him

And what about my dream
Of us in Amsterdam?
He had a blond buzz haircut
And white T-shirt
And the man
Walking down the street in Laguna
Had a blond buzz haircut
And white T-shirt!'

'That's not proof it was him
Probably a mere coincidence.'

'It's *magical* proof
To me anyway
Perhaps it was him
And he was visiting Laguna
In the dream we were in Amsterdam
So maybe that is where we meet
And more importantly
I also know what he feels like—
His peaceful vibration—
And *that!*
That alone
Is worth attempting the impossible
You see, Mr. Head

Nothing
Before or since
Has felt like being in Angel's arms.'

That's the name I gave you
That's what you felt like
An Amsterdam Angel

Safe
Warm
Peaceful
Erotic
Sensual
Loving
All rolled into one feeling

'Mr. Head it *is* worth trying
For *that* feeling
It is all that I need
Because *the* dream of all dreams
More than Australia
Or a café in England
Is love
It overrules them all
That was the *whole point* of coming out
To have love
And share my life with someone openly
What was the point of the *struggle*
But to be with the right love?'

And I knew whom I shared it with
With you
I just had to find you

*

So after Labor Day
When the tourists faded away

19

I was on a plane to Amsterdam for a week
A tiny detour
From one dream to another
For love
Just to see
If fate would bring
You
To me again

On the flight over
I played a mixed CD
Made for me by a friend
Then snuggled into a state
Between awake and asleep
A song began that I had never heard
The Promise
By Tracy Chapman
So beautiful!
It spoke to *exactly* what I was doing
In coming back to Amsterdam
Coming back for you
I designated it as a song for us
To think of you whenever I heard it

I played it over and over again
Carried on the words' sentiment
Across the ocean
Like a magic carpet ride

"If you wait for me
Then I'll come for you
Although I've traveled far
I always hold
A place for you
In my heart..."

Oh, I was *so* positive we would reunite!
The song was a *great* sign to me

*

Well
One week turned into a month
I didn't get back on my plane to California
I couldn't
I hadn't found you
I had been staying at the Globe Hostel
Near Centraal Station
Where Mike and I stayed
Our first time in Amsterdam

I wanted more privacy
Now that I was there longer
I rented a little apartment
Near Leidseplein
Above a chic café
Called Aroma
It's now a Walk-to-Wok

I would have breakfast
Crush on the waiter
And get in-tune to your aroma
Go where I felt like going
Do what I felt like doing
All the while keeping an eye out for you
Any blond hair, blue-eyed boys
Of a certain age
That I passed on the street
Or saw through a restaurant window
I would take a second look
Sometimes a third
Just to be sure if it was you or not

*

Oh yes, I went to Cockring
The first day I arrived

20

After the clock struck midnight
I thought the magic would continue
Where it started
So I was there
Zipping through the club
And the darkroom
It was that first night
I met my friend Art
I described you to him

"Blond hair, blue-eyes, huh?
You realize that's the majority
Of Dutch men in Holland,"
He said with a smile.

"I know," I replied.

"I'll keep an eye out for him," he said.
We've been friends ever since

*

As the month went on
I had to find another home
One night I was at a club
Near Rembrandtplein
I saw a man across the dance floor
His eyes sparkled
With the flashing disco lights
I thought it was you!
I *hoped* it was you!
My heart felt light at the possibility
We playfully flirted
As we came closer through the crowd
To the center of the dance floor
Where I realized
It wasn't you
But I felt swept away

And before I knew it
I was on the back of his bike
Going home with him
Along the ride
I shared with him a bit about myself
And mentioned
My need for a new home

"Come stay with me!"
Nick said instantly.

As we rode across a canal bridge
While the street lamps
Danced on the water
It was romantic
But the next morning
I felt bad
For hoping he was someone else
You
Then simply left back to my flat

I moved into another hostel
It started to get cold and wet
As autumn began
I was feeling rundown
From all the searching
I was disappointed and sad
I felt silly, foolish really
For trying to find you
I had romanticized it so much
And when you didn't appear
Well... I thought,
'It's *my* turn
For something beautiful.'
I hadn't learned the lesson yet
Life doesn't owe me anything
It gives and it takes

So I decided
I had to give love—
Or the possibility of it
A chance
I owed that to myself
Even if it wasn't... you

I was cold, tired and lonely
And there was a man
I had laughter and playfulness with
I needed that
After looking for you

*

One rainy afternoon
I left the hostel and went to a museum
The one Nick mentioned he worked at
When the woman let me pass through
Without paying
I was a bit confused
I began in the first room
While attempting to dry off—
No umbrella—
When I turned around
Nick was standing there
He noticed me on the security camera
And quickly radioed the ticket woman
To let me through
It was charming

I was afraid to ask
If his invitation still stood
The way I had left his home that morning
But I didn't have to
When I left he grabbed an umbrella
Offered it and his home
And took in this wet stray cat

*

After that first month
Amsterdam became
A home base for my travels
Where they had their beginning
And end

Instead of returning to California
I bought a round trip
From Amsterdam to Michigan
When I returned to my family
My heart felt broken
It confused me
How could I have a broken heart?
For a man I knew nothing about
But I did
And I did know something about you
You are gentle
Peaceful
Loving
The rest is semantics
My heart ached, *physically* ached
Because I thought we would meet
I wanted to apologize
For lying about my name
And having a place to go that night
I trusted you would understand
But even more so
My heart broke
Because I couldn't *tell* you
That *yes!*
Our time together
Was very special for me too!
What a precious gift
A remarkable gesture
A beautiful man
Thank you

All of it
I couldn't tell you

While my experience of you
Was of an angel of light and love
I was saddened that yours of me
At least the last impression
Was an angel of darkness and fear
I knew I had a lot of love to give
My heart broke
Because the one I wanted to give it to
Was you

Through that sadness a song was
channeled
About meeting you
The experience
Had to be immortalized in art
That
Was when you began
As my muse
Unbeknownst to me
How endlessly you would be

*

While visiting my family
I settled on my plan—
Australia and a café in England
I returned to Amsterdam for a few days
Before leaving for Australia
And stayed with Nick again
We got along well
Laughed a lot
But skipped straight
To no-sex companionship
We'd cuddle for a few minutes
Each night before sleep

He amused me and confused me
We had this thing
Where we would ask the other
"Say something sweet"
And we did
Ohhhh, he was *good* at it!
He would say the most *beautiful* things
And I would be hooked

We played house
And I was grateful to him
It was nice to be in a home
And lie next to someone
I was open to changing my plans
Turn our make-believe
Into something real
But Nick didn't want to go there

*

So
I went to Australia
To learn my friends' hearts
Weren't in the cafe anymore
That was my New Year's news
After meeting up with them
At a club in Sydney
Just after midnight

It seemed nine months prior
Anything felt possible *and* exciting!
Now as they approached
The end of their travels
Jobs were needed for debt incurred
Enjoying their time around the world
My heart sank and a streak of...
Uh-oh-what-do-I-do-now
Shot through me

But I understood, of course
I loved them
The ecstasy Emma popped into my mouth
As soon as we met up helped
Come to think of it
We were rolling on 'e'
At the club in Hollywood
When the dream that I was now in
Was birthed

I had to laugh
How could I not
I had stuff in Laguna and Amsterdam
My body was in Sydney
And I was trying to start a café in England —
Minus the two partners—
But in that moment
It was all a no-worry-world away
With nothing left to do
But dance

I tried to see it as a catalyst
For something else
Maybe
There was a new life for me in Australia
Or perhaps *you* were in Australia
If you could be in Laguna
Anything was possible
Didn't hurt to take a good look
At any blond hair, blue-eyed men
From Sydney to Melbourne to Perth
While creating my own
Experience Down Under

*

I left the sweltering
Summer heat of Perth

And after two days of traveling
Arrived at Nick's door
In the bitter cold winter of Amsterdam
I don't think I've ever been so tired
Or *freezing!*
I didn't know which end was up
While waiting for Nick outside
To get back from work
Days and time had no meaning
As I readjusted to spinning
In the Northern Hemisphere

One week in Amsterdam
Turned into two
I didn't know what to do
About the café dream in England
But procrastinate

My heart went back to you
Perhaps that dream
Still had a shot
It worked out well
How Amsterdam became
The home base of my travels
So I kept an eye out
Before reluctantly going to Oxford

*

In the interim
I discovered on-line dating
With a site called Gaydar
Did you ever have a profile on Gaydar?
I had one for years
Screen name: Magicpowers
Password: AmsAngel
Of course
That is why I created a profile

24

It was my next light bulb moment
Another way!
The way!
To find you

Chat rooms and profiles
In Amsterdam and the Netherlands
Were searched
I was certain
That
Would be the way I found you
Technology made everything easier
Why not for this
But I didn't see you
In the virtual world either

I used the site more in my travels
It wasn't that big in America
But I met wonderful friends
Nice dates, wild dates, homes and jobs
And yes
Some sex too
It was a great resource

*

I met a man from Oxford in a chatroom
He gave me work
Bar-backing, club promoting,
And hosting in a friend's restaurant
Above the bar
To learn about the business

It was a great experience
I regretted not coming out sooner
In college at least
To have the simple pleasures
Of emotional development

Exploring love's firsts
Before innocence is lost
First date
First kiss
First love
With the gender you knew
You wanted it with
And *no* trauma
Figuring it out
Wow
What a concept
Yes, I *did* wish I had that life experience

Instead of school dances and Valentines
With a boy
Red Light District, porn, and parks
Were my intro
Well, yes, I did have a first love
You
Unconventional as it was
Because I couldn't ask your name
Or anything about you
So Oxford gave a tiny taste
Of being out at university
There were men from all over the world
I was the new, older guy—
At twenty-seven—in town
And the boys were friendly and welcoming

But a month later
One night working in the restaurant
Being very present
I realized
Here I was
In my café in Europe
It wasn't "mine"
But I was in the experience
Dreamt of months ago in Hollywood

Albeit changed along the way
But I'd made my unknown known
The dream felt accomplished
And it wasn't what I wanted anymore
My friends weren't a part of it
My heart's dream
Was originally in Amsterdam
The café and you
That was the ideal combination

So with love on my brain
I stopped in Amsterdam
En route to Laguna
To take one more pull
On the slot machine
Hoping to hit the Angel jackpot!
But no triple 7's came up
So I returned
To Laguna's paradise bubble

*

"I'd been around the world
And I, I, I, I couldn't find my baby."
But I would have traded the world
To meet you

I was inspired though
With you as my muse again
To begin writing the story
Of a man searching for a man
He knows nothing about
Except his eyes
His smile
And what he feels like

I grabbed a notebook and pen
The story *flew* out of me

Until the ending
Ideally it was to meet you
Yes, it could have an existential ending
About the search for self and all that
But it felt like
There was more to the story
So I put it away
Sank into Laguna's healing energy
To work its magic
As summer approached

I found a charming home in the village
Began bartending—
I *had* studied at Oxford—
At Main Street
A gay cabaret bar
Next door to the Klatch
Working the karaoke nights

I didn't know what dream to dream next
I hadn't thought about a *next* dream—
Other than you
Or that I would need one

*

South Africa had been big on my list
A twenty-year curiousity
I decided to set a goal:
Save for a year
Go for three months
See what there was to experience
And go from there

Ray
A friend I met in Laguna
Was from Cape Town
He was a good resource to ask questions

And my excitement grew
But by the end of summer
I met a man from Iran
On the dance floor of the Boom Boom Room
I was hooked
His shirt said "Lover"
And I thought OK.
The Africa dream flew out the window
For a dream of love
Or the possibility of it
Always the first priority
After experiencing it with you
It was a no-brainer
To make love the goal

*

Not long after Iran and I parted ways
And that possibility ended
I was in San Francisco
And met an erotic photographer
Biron
He spoke of photography
And the male form
With passion I respected
One artist to another

When he offered to do a shoot
My clothes came off
With the erections of framed models
On the surrounding walls

It was intimately creative
Providing a new outlet and medium
For me from writing
Exploring fashion and photography
I had ideas
And Biron was open to collaboration

The experience helped release so much
Shed a skin
And opened me up for *something*
A new chapter
Somewhere

*

After the third shoot
I showed the pictures to Ray
When I finished
In one swift motion
He made me stand
Grabbed his tape measure
Knelt before me
With one end on the ground
And rose the other to my crotch

"Oh! What are you doing?"

"Taking your measurements
For your zed card
And we'll add a few of these photos."

"What is a zed card?"

"For modeling."

"Modeling?
What are you talking about?"

"Anthony, these photos are great!
I want you to promise me
You're going to print up a card
And send them out to agencies."

"But…"

"No more buts—
I've seen enough of yours
Promise me."

"I promise."

I thought maybe it could be
A stepping-stone to something else
What?
I had no idea
I *was* craving change
I considered a move up the coast to L.A.

So I did as Ray suggested
Printed fifty zed cards
Looked up agencies around the world
And sent them out

I didn't put much faith in it
Especially when rejections
Started coming in
From nearly every continent
Asia...rejected
Paris...rejected
London...rejected
L.A...rejected
New York!...
...*Rejected!*

*

Then one day
A response of interest arrived in my inbox
From *Cape Town*!
I hadn't thought about
My South Africa dream
Since I met Iran Man
Now the dream

I sent flying out the window
Nearly a year before
Flew back in via email
A man from an agency in Cape Town
Invited me there
I didn't know what to do
Ray encouraged me
To just say...
"Yes!"

*

Soon after, I had a dream of you
A *stunning* image
Both the scenery and *you!*
It felt *so good* to be with you again
Alone
With private, intimate time
Me and you

We were on a *spectacular*
Rocky coast of Africa
You were in white
And looked...
Sooo beautiful!
There were candles *everywhere*
On the rocks and cliffs
Hundreds
From the sea to the highest cliff
Something that could *never* be achieved
In real life
Candles, everywhere, staying lit
As the waves crashed
An image that could *only* happen
In a dream

It was really romantic!
And sooo peaceful

There
With you
A *radiant* image!
You were smiling that beautiful smile—
Like the last time I saw you in Cockring—
Laughing and excited to hear
All of the adventures I had
Since we were last together
Like Odysseus reuniting with Penelope
You were a muse
And now like a guide
The *sexiest* guide I'd ever seen
I took it as a sign to commit to Africa
And began to dismantle my life
In Laguna for a second time

*

Right before I left for Africa
I had *another* dream of you
I was in Amsterdam
Walking to Centraal Station
There were many people
Heading in the same direction
Then
I saw you
Out of my peripheral vision
You noticed me
And we gravitated toward each other
Until we were side by side
We didn't speak
But *knew* it was the other
And instead of going to the station
I veered right
With your lead
Still never talking
Felt *so good* knowing it was you
And that you knew

It was I
A *very* happy dream
You led me toward a canal
Then to a houseboat
Your houseboat
You opened the cabin and went in
As I followed you
I had the feeling
I was home
Then woke up

*

By October I was off
First to Amsterdam
I was conscious
Of not turning Amsterdam
Into another search for you
Feelings of foolishness lingered

Yes
I did go to Cockring for fun
And I did have a look around for you
In the darkroom
On the dance floor
Sometimes, in the dark
I would feel the vibration of someone
That felt *soooo* similar to you
My heart would begin beating faster
Wondering
If it was indeed
You
But then...*something*
And I knew it wasn't
And I had to leave
It was both hauntingly beautiful
Then hauntingly
Haunting

As if your ghost brushed me
For a moment

I left Cockring early in the morning
Returned to my hotel for my bags
And walked toward Centraal Station
To catch my train to the airport
Yes, the dream *was* on my mind
Perhaps it was a prophetic dream
I did take a scan of the area
As I approached the station
I would have dropped Africa
In an instant for a date
Had I seen you
But, I did not
So, I flew to Cape Town
I *was* open to starting a new life there
If one presented itself

*

When I arrived
I went to see the man from the agency
I had been corresponding with
He was on sabbatical
Nobody at the agency
Was aware of our discussion
I left my zed card
And told them to contact me
If work came up
But my gut said
It was a dead end
I tried to remain positive
That it was a catalyst to get me there
For something else

Then wandered into the City Center
Toward Greenmarket Square

A *lively* African market selling crafts
I felt lonely...and scared
Confused what to do next
I thought the electricity
Of the market would help

As I approached a booth selling CDs
I heard a song playing
And froze with shock
As Tracy's voice floated through the air
Singing *The Promise*
The words filling my heart

"If you
Think of me
If you miss me
Once in awhile
Then I'll return
To you
I'll return
And fill
That space
In your heart."

And I *did!*
Miss you in that moment!
And *felt* you
Fill that space in my heart
I was overwhelmed and dizzy
From the *longing*
Of love
Of you
Filling that space between my arms

And then
I put one foot in front of the other
I signed with another agency
Found a home

30

Along with a *colorful*
Artistic group of friends
Everything from that point
Had come together rather effortlessly
It helped me feel I was *right*
Where I was suppose to be
For that moment in time

*

Not long after I moved into my flat
I had a dream of you that woke me
We were naked in bed
You behind me
With your arms wrapped around me
Felt so good to lean into you
Be held by you
Me, filling that space
Between *your* arms
A loving and peaceful way to wake up!
And as promised
Whenever you appeared
—In thought or dream —
Love was sent your way

*

As I began adjusting to Cape Town
And the industry
I learned the season of advertisers
And models
Was prime after the holidays
That's how I ended up extending my visa
From three months
To six
All being charged
On six credit cards

Yes it gave anxiety
But I did trust
That I was brought there for *something*
And inspiration came
Again with you
It began with lyrics and poems
I dabbled with some scenes of a screenplay
Beginning at Cockring
The first night of the search
And meeting Art
It felt blissful
So I followed the bliss

*

My friends were artistic too
We would have salon sessions
Sharing and creating art
It was at one of these salons
Dawn asked
Where my inspiration came from
I said you, of course
But was hesitant to share
The search for you
Doing so would trigger
Bitter sweetness
I felt I had to let it go
Mr. Head was probably right
It was nearly *impossible*
To find you

I thought I had to "grow-up"
Stop chasing after one man
Give others a chance
And I *did*...I *really* did!
From California to Europe to Australia
And to, yes, now Cape Town
But...

"Nothing compares
Nothing compares to you."

But I shared our experience with Dawn
Including the search that followed
She was touched by the story
And the love you expressed

While Dawn and I chatted
Francois, who hosted the salons
Put on a CD
Guess what he chose
Yup, Tracy Chapman
The Promise
Came floating through
As we were talking about you

"If you
Dream of me
Like I
Dream of you
In a place that's warm
And dark
In a place where I
Can feel
The beating
Of your heart."

I asked Francois why he put it on
He said he loved Tracy
So I shared our story with him
And you continued as my muse
It was working
I was writing…
Why mess with a good thing?
Makes me laugh to this day
Thinking of how many people
Around the *world* over the years

Have heard about you
Whether they wanted to or not

*

I did do a few castings
For Dutch companies
One a lottery ad
The other a beer commercial
I thought, *maybe*
You would catch me on TV
And investigate
Or see my face
In a print ad on the streets
Or passing you on a bus

But I wasn't very good at the modeling
I didn't have "It"
Or if I did
I didn't turn it on at the right time
But I tried
And *every* casting
Pushed me through a little fear
Of even trying
Between beach, salons, and castings
I still had a lot of time
So, I continued to write

*

You appeared *even* in the bush
When I went on safari
Our group arrived at a campground
In a little town called Palapye, Botswana
Myself and one of the Dutch men
Went with our guide for supplies
Into the town center
It consisted of a gas station and a market

32

The market was lively with people
There were Cabbage Patch dolls
Lined across the top of the meat cooler
You could grab your 80's nostalgia
And your meat in one swoop
When we stood in line
A woman with large breasts
Had a bright pink T-shirt on
That said ANGEL
Her breasts expanding the letters
Like balloons
Floating into my face
Of course you came to my mind
So thoughts of love
Were sent your way
On that Christmas Eve
And for me
It was holiday magic
The way you came
To my mind and heart
In Botswana

*

After the holiday
I settled further into a Cape Townian life
I continued to explore
Different types of writing
I *liked* the idea
Of a man searching for a man
He knows nothing about
But I didn't know how
To end it or begin it

"Every story has a hero
And he wants one thing"
I had the story
I had the hero

But the hero
And the desire
Were the same thing
And I didn't meet you yet
So it felt like the story
Was in a holding pattern

*

When the season drew to a close
My agent suggested
I stay in the cycle
And gave recommendations
Of agencies in Italy
He thought I'd be a match with
And had connections
Sure it sounded exciting
But I would have to *survive* until autumn
And the credit cards would *long*
Be maxed out by then

I did get one job!
For a Swiss billboard
With a *check*
Next to international supermodel
It was time to move on
I thought I'd regroup in Laguna
But *not* before!
A 30_{th} birthday present to myself
What else?
Ten days!
In Amsterdam
I *was* already...I don't know
$15,000 in debt
What was another $1,000?

*

33

Dawn and I climbed Table Mountain
Days before I left Cape Town
I was sharing my decision
To go to Amsterdam

I wanted advice on how to approach it
I was hesitant of it turning into
A search for you again
Feelings of foolishness *still* lingered

Her advice
Stand in a favorite spot
For me
It is the star at the center of Leidseplein
I actually feel I saw you on it
Those twenty years ago
And while I'm standing there
Send out a *blast!*
Of love
She assured me you would receive it
Along with thoughts of an invitation
If you had time to meet
Then go about enjoying my time
In Amsterdam
And I did
Amsterdam was my runway on my 30th
Art and I had *such* fun dancing
He's a great dancer
And *fun* to dance with
It was so nice to be there in spring
Everything was starting to bloom
Including myself
Yeah, I was thousands of dollars in debt
But I was happy
The dream conceived in Laguna
Nearly two years prior
To just go to Africa for three months
And see what was there
Doubled to six

I saw the experience through
And what was there…
Was a *beautiful* African family

I pushed through fears
Of learning and trying modeling
Had adventures around the bush with lions
With playful gentlemen callers—
African Ambassadors—sprinkled in
And so much more
That is what was there for me
A life created
In Africa
The dream turned bigger
Then I ever imagined in Laguna
As they say
Everything is bigger in Africa
But most importantly
The unexpected discovery
Was you
Meeting me there
Collaborating together in art
You bringing the inspiration
Me writing
Me and you

Mejou!

All of it made me soar
Into higher dimensions
For doing something
That *really* scared me
In the beginning
And with a new decade approaching
It was a time
To *celebrate!*

*

One morning
I woke in my flat
The 9th of May to be exact
As I lied in bed
Thoughts of you floated
As if they drifted through the windows
And blanketed me
So I thought
Ok
Good morning Sir
This is a lovely, unexpected surprise
But *so* welcomed
Especially
In that state between awake and dream
When your body naturally wakes up
Because it's had enough rest
And you feel
Sooo cozy
Always such a nice place to meet you—
And in the morning
Of a sun-filled new day

*

I decided
Since you came to wake me up
I would dedicate the day to us
And imagine what it would be like
To spend a day with you
Whether in person or my imagination
I think we forget to use it as we get older
So I used mine
First, well, yes
I did masturbate
It was as *hot* as I remember
Then, while I made breakfast
And contemplated what to do with the day
I looked out the window for the weather

Beautiful!
De park! Vondelpark
Perfect spring day for it

The trees that lined the path
Leading into the park
Were in *full* bloom and color
There were many people enjoying the day
Having picnics, playing catch, and laughing
Soaking up the light like sunflowers

I found a nice spot near the pond
Laid my blanket down
And lied on my back
Ohhhh, It felt *so* good
To have my *entire b*ody on the ground
I had been traveling around so much
Continent to continent to continent
Hemisphere to hemisphere
But when I lied on the earth in Vondel
I felt *all of* Mother Nature supporting me
I was happy

I felt *completely* at home in Mother Nature…
In my body
And it was a pleasure to share such bliss
With you in my imagination
Lying next to me
Cuddling
It all added to the joy
I was sure of it
I was in my perfect vision of heaven

*

An hour later
I walked the path along the pond
It led into an area covered by trees

When I came out on the other side
My attention was drawn to the left
Toward a fountain in the middle of the water
And beyond it
To a tree on the opposite side with shade
That was my next spot

As I turned my head straight forward
I did so in just enough time
To catch a glimpse
Of a man with blond hair
And a flash of eyes
A vibration...an aura
Showered me with familiarity

By the time the message reached my head
And I turned for a second look
Gray pants and brown shoes
Short-sleeve collard pullover
Gray and white stripes
With one of, I think red
Yes I thought
It could be
It feels like...

I waited to see
If the man would do a second look
I had a moment of insecurity
The type that can be erased
When that second look occurs
Because it is mutual *and* simultaneous

He didn't look
Or if he did, not when I did
Either way I felt insecure
My current situation
Of debt, no job, and no home
Triggered my insecurity

What did I have to offer?
Had too much time passed?
Maybe he didn't wonder about me
Like I wondered about him

Then the man seemed to...float
Diagonally
Onto the same path I had just walked
Like a car slowly veering out of its lane
As if he was lost in thought
Then he disappeared
Into the tree-covered path
Well, that time
I really thought I hallucinated you
It was more of an energy experience
Passing through me
And the way he appeared to float
I questioned if you were real
Or if I imagined
Our whole experience together

But then the tinge of sadness
Came flooding back
From the initial search
The *foolishness* that always lingered
Chasing after
A second chance with first love
Or at *least* to know your name
Erase the Land of Misfits Toy feeling
That something was wrong with me
Abnormal
Stupid
As the toy that didn't know
His first love's name
But what do you say?
It all seemed so outer body
The day
I imagine us spending *together*

Experiencing
What I envision my heaven to be
With you in it
And then you appear
My heaven's Angel?
I felt I really was in a sprookje
But forgot I was one of the leading men

Yes!
I kicked myself all the way back to America
For not saying, "Hello, I feel we've met."
Something

*

I returned to my family
For an autumn to spring gestation
After one last summer in Laguna
Realizing
The "California Dream" chapter of my life
Was complete

When I arrived, it *struck* me
I had my story...
You
I wrote the story of meeting you
Of searching for you
And all the dreams along the way
The sighting in Laguna
The inspiration in Africa
Your evolvement into my muse
Ending...with meeting you in the park
In my heaven

*

The plan was...
The book would

You know
Land in front of Oprah
Be chosen for her book club
And have people also wondering
Like myself

Who is Amsterdam Angel?

Or land in front of *your* eyes
And you'd be like:
"Hey! He's writing about me!"
And then you'd contact me
That was my next plan
Of how to find you
I felt a creative surge
It felt *blissful*
You continued as my muse
And became The Dutch Prince
Of de sprookje

*

Ohhhh, I had a lot of drive for writing
I *believed* in the story
I *believed* in a happy reunion
I *believed* in sharing
A beautiful love story
Between two men
Writing into existence
The story I didn't know *could* exist
When I was growing up
Righting that wrong
For those needing it *now*
Like I needed it *then*
For more peace to their hearts and minds
Then I
And countless people before me had
In discovering who

They desired to love
And showcasing
An incredible man
You

Then my love for you
Became more remarkable to me
And deepened
Even without interacting
For six years
Because you gave me
My dream of writing a book
By giving me the story
With you as the shining star
It was very magical to me
So I sent gratitude and love to you
For making a dream come true

*

By spring
A new seed began sprouting
In the garden of my life
An opportunity to bartend was presented
In a little town called Provincetown,
At The Crown and Anchor
You had taught me to stay open
To *anything*
Life would take it from there

While I worked on a third draft
Whispers of you followed me to P-town
Whether a tourist sitting at my bar
Was from or talking about Amsterdam
Or seeing the word angel around town
Or hearing it in songs
It all made me think of you
And, as promised

I'd send love your way

With the end of summer
Carnival Week came around
The theme that year was...fairy tales
Ohhhh, it was when P-town
Really dove into its imagination
With parties every night
Different costumes
I watched it all from behind the bar
As the lively characters
Of many fairy tales
Came to *life!*
While my imagination drifted
To another fairy tale
Nobody had heard of...
Yet

It was the start of an idea
I had no idea
Where it was going to take me

*

It was carnival day that I realized
I *had* to do
Something else with my life
In thinking of you
In thinking of Amsterdam
I thought
I'm simply going to figure out a way
To be there more
Yes, I reconciled
I would *always* dream
Of wanting to meet you again
While realizing life
Is going on for you too

You may have met someone
And be happy in another life
But at least a meet
I would always wish
And yes, if you were single
And curious
A date
And until that happened
I would live in the place that *always*
Made me feel happy
Much to do
With the fairy tale with you

But also
With the canals, bridges, and houses
And the melting pot of lively characters
Amsterdam is *always*
Quirky and charming magic to me
Playful, silly, and sexy
The perfect medieval fairy tale set
Preserved in time
And mixed with modern touches
Like rendezvous in clubs like Cockring

I decided to be a flight attendant
Take a Dutch course
Work Amsterdam flights
And be bi-continental
That was my next plan

*

By the end of the year
A third draft was completed
I left for Amsterdam for three months
To learn Dutch
And yes
Ninety-some days

To, perhaps, bump into you
Was a bonus
But I never did

Before I returned to America
Joakim Karlsson
A Swedish photographer
Reached out to me on Gaydar
He was creating a book
Photographing fifty men in fifty cities
He asked if I would be
His Amsterdam Man
I told him thank you
But I was returning to America
He mentioned
He would be touring the States
In a few weeks
Then asked if I would like to meet him
In New York City
It was an exciting offer
New York and I still had not met
But my focus was on applying to airlines
And getting a job
The interview that presented itself
Was not an international airline
But a brand new domestic one
Virgin America

They only had five destinations
The closest to Michigan was New York
I needed to get to San Francisco
For the interview
Luckily the timing was perfect
To meet the Swedish photographer
Do the shoot
Then fly to San Francisco

I flew into JFK late and went to Brooklyn

To meet Mike's brother
Who was living there with his wife
Again, like in Amsterdam eight years prior
Zack provided me with a home

Early the next morning
I met the photographer
At 110$_{th}$ and Amsterdam
We went up to the rooftop
I took off my clothes
And Manhattan and I
Were introduced
After the shoot
I walked through Central Park
To Columbus Circle
Before catching the subway
To the village to meet Tom
A friend of a friend
Who let me stay with him
The park was perfectly in bloom
The city put me under its spell
I fell in love
But the job would have me move
To San Francisco

When I stepped onto my flight
To fly west for the interview
There she was!
Sitting in first class!
Tracy Chapman!
Reminding me of
The Promise I made
Giddy with excitement
I waited for Ms. Chapman
Outside the gate
I *had* to tell her
How special the song was to me
She was very gracious

Her presence
An inaudible whisper
Reminding me

Don't forget your promise

I was hired for the job
The first day of my training
They announced a new base opening
In New York
And asked for volunteers
My hand shot up

After I completed my training
I flew back to the city
Tom graciously provided my first home
While I settled into the tiny island
Of New Amsterdam

I stayed with Tom for my first year
Before finding my home
Where I've lived ever since
Here on 19$_{th}$ street
Where *you* came walking down today!

*

Part II

Anthony and Angel
Begin walking down 19th Street
Heading west towards the Hudson
To go sit on the grass
At Christopher St. Pier.

As I began setting up my new life
I felt it was time to love and let go
Of the dream of meeting you
Give the opportunity
Presented to me a chance
I doubted a book could find you
And that idea got shelved

Feelings of foolishness remained
Of trying to find someone with a book
Who does that?
No, really, I wanted to know
Needed to know
If there was *someone* in the world
Who had a guidebook of their experience
But there was none

I tried to block it out
To forgo the book
The dream
You
As I navigated creating a home
In the city and the skies
But thoughts of you would *always*
Find their way to me
Somehow, someway
Usually when I tried to let go

Once, shortly after I moved to Manhattan
I was invited to an art sale
There was a small and simple
Yet beautifully poignant piece entitled:
'Two People Waiting To Meet'
By Ed Ruscha, if I remember correctly
With one person on one side
And another on the other
When *boom* you came to mind
And the longing I felt to meet you

It had me lost staring at it for...
I don't know how long
Until a woman came up to me
And commented on it as well
To encourage a sale
Referring to what a good price it was
At $2500
I would have loved to purchase it
Felt it was a piece of you
Of us
When I looked at it
But it cost an eighth
Of my first year flight attendant salary
I told her I agreed
But then excused myself
And continued to try and let go
Of the wanting
The waiting
To meet *you*

*

I kept my gig in Provincetown
Just a couple weeks in the summer
During the busiest times
To be an extra hand
And visit the home and family
That Provincetown & The Crown had become
It was just over a year later
That like *many* before me
I met a love in P-town
I owed it to myself
Someone was offering me committment
It felt right
He was kind
And I loved him

Dante received my love

In the ways that I wanted to show it
He was *very* encouraging of my writing
I was hesitant and torn
Yes, I enjoyed it
But the purpose was to find you
And I was in a relationship now
Maybe writing was just for me
To heal through reflection
I had a dream to write a book
Make my unknown known
And I had
So I continued to try and let go
Of that dream
And of you

*

Early on in our relationship
A tragedy struck
The loss of a chosen younger brother
From my chosen family in Laguna
His father, a dear friend
And the owner of both my first home
And place of work in Laguna
At the Koffee Klatch
Again that traumatic shock
Of someone *very* young
Gone
Just like that

It's powerful how broken hearts
Can feel so different and distinct
With Joe it felt as if my heart
Was frozen in dry ice
Which burned at the slightest touch
Electrically shocked occasionally
With travel or drugs—
Any new stimulation

To my eyes and body
With Mohammad
My heart crumbled like a porcelain vase
Every time he came to mind
When these things happen
It's hard not to wonder
How could this happen?
It happens so fast and eerily quiet—
Simply slipping away to the other side

*

Every time my work brought me to L.A.
I would go to Laguna
To be there for Sam
The way Mike was there for me
Through Joe's death
Laguna
This *beautiful* paradise
Now overshadowed by sadness

But my beck-and-call
Availability to Sam
By phone or in person
Put a strain on my relationship
It took time away from it
And Dante felt shut out
It wasn't intentional
The darkness and heaviness
I experienced through Sam
Was indescribable
Chilling to hear his thoughts
As I walked with him
Through the loss of an only child
I *had* to be there for Sam
I had trouble understanding
How did Dante not
Just understand that?

I was equally blind to Dante's perspective
And we broke up for a couple of months

I went to Europe
To reconnect with friends
Ray had married a German man
And was living in Munich
I visited him in autumn
Then returned to Amsterdam in December
To visit Art
It had been over four years
Since I'd been there

Yes, of *course,* I thought of you
It was ten years to the month
That we met
The snow twinkled down softly
Like it had back then

*

One evening
I wandered on Warmoesstraat
A stroll down memory lane to Cockring
To honor the milestone of when we met
And send a dose of love and gratitude

When I arrived
It was all boarded up!
Closed!
The letters spelling Cockring torn off
I couldn't believe it
So much so
That the next night I decided to go back
Just to make sure I hadn't imagined it
Nope, out of business
End of an era
My head trying to convince my heart

It was a clear sign to let go
More so as Dante and I had decided
To give our relationship another chance
Upon my return from Amsterdam

As I drew closer
I saw a group of men and women
Standing in front of the old club
One man was speaking to the others

"Now,
"We're standing in front
Of what *used* to be the *Cockring.*"

From there I heard bits and pieces
About sex and drugs
And realized
It was a stop on a tour!
The guide was putting
A Studio 54 spin to the Cockring story!
Well, yes
Sex and drugs did go on there
But two people
Once upon a December
Had an enchanting experience there
Proving that love could be found
In *the most*
Unexpected place

*

That could be the opening scene
Ten years later: a tour stop
Me
Standing in front
Of the boarded up club
Wondering
If it really happened

Or if it *was* a fable
Which I *did* wonder...for a moment
As the idea from Provincetown's
Fairy tale carnival seed
Began budding
With a fabled hero
A sexy rescue worker
Jumping into the darkness
Heralding love and light
Shining brightness again
Rekindling my spark
With that of his own

*

I thought I had my ending
Finally
And in doing so, inspiration bubbled
Encouragement from Dante resumed
And in the following year
Channeling my grief
And love for Mohammad
I was inspired to split the original book
Into a series
Memoir morphing into a fairy tale—
For adults

I surfed the joy
Feeling creative and challenged
Carried by the wave
Along with the renewed love
And support of a partner

The goal date
12-12-12
Was met
The first book
Amsterdam Angel

Was in the world
It covered childhood,
Going through Joe's death
The beginning of exploring my sexuality
And ended with how we met

The launch was a success
And raised money
For the Ali Forney Center
Which was hit hard
By Hurricane Sandy weeks before—
With only weeks to plan
My wizard friend Addam
Whipped the event together
With a wave of his wand
Like magic
Even getting a celebrity appearance—
Lea DeLaria
Whom, I admit
I wasn't all that familiar with at the time

"So what are you working on now?"
I asked Lea at the launch
She said she just completed filming
The first season of a new series
About a women's prison
And BOOM
Not long after
Everybody was familiar
With Lea DeLaria

*

I began going to Amsterdam to write
Art was my patron
He gave me a room in his home
And space to work
I was able to have a month or two off

Each year
I accomplished my original dream
Being bi-continental
In the fairy tale set of Amsterdam

*

Shortly before a writing period
The following autumn
I was injured in an accident
Dante and I
Were going through a rough patch
Along with the flying
My writing
Took me out of the city even more
But putting an ocean
Between everything in America
And my writing
Helped me drop into the story
And kick it out

Now the injury
Would put more stress
On our relationship
As I learned to manage pain
And still be an active adult

When I left for Amsterdam
We needed space
The month I was away
Was precious time
I felt bliss and happiness
Working on something I loved

*

The second day I was there
The 25th of October 2013

To be exact
I began the morning and day
Organizing and writing
By late afternoon I needed a break
To get out of my head ...
The Carnival!
I saw it was back the day before

Every now and then
It appears like magic
In front of the Royal Palace
The last time I had seen it
Was before I left for Cape Town
Eight years prior

I *love* it!
It evokes a happy innocence
Where people remember to play
With rides and games
Bells and whistles
Laughter, screams
And people flying through the air

It made me happy
When the carnival and I
Were in town together
It was perfect to get out
Of the two-dimensional world of writing
And rejoin the third

After strolling around
Taking in the lively energy
I approached one of the booths
Selling sweet treats
And ordered a chocolate waffle
Then stepped to the side
To wait as it was warmed
It was a bit crowded

I felt someone brush against me
Squeezing through to the counter
To place their order
Just from behind
I could feel *the* vibration

*

The man came up to the counter
As the woman handed me my waffle
I glanced
Yes, dirty blond hair
And a glimpse of blue eye
That felt familiar
I moved out of the way
To allow the next person up
And went to stand
Near the side of the square
To eat my waffle
Moments later I scanned the area
And saw the man ten meters away
He had a brown coat on and jeans
The hair was longer
But yes
Adding now thirteen years
That
Could be
Angel

Well
From the darkroom of Cockring
All those years ago
To its extreme
A joyous and laughter filled Carnival
Had me turned inside out
And split into two universes
The one I had created in another land...
With another man

And the one with the man of my dreams —
Quite literally
Possibly standing ten meters away?
I felt swept up in a carnival world
Of illusions and realms

Yes Dante and I were on a break
But I felt a loyalty to the relationship
To either end it
Or continue it

But standing *so* close
Was a dream from long ago
You
I was time traveling between the two lives
I didn't know what was happening
I oscillated betwixt the two realms
The present seemed but a flash
In the middle of them both
Like the rides spinning above me
In those glimpses of connection
With the man's eyes
They were filled with light
And the brief flash of them
Seemed to say
Yes! It is me!
Come!

*

I knew I had to go to him
Since I walked away the first time
After a few moments of flashbacks
To Dante and New York
The darkroom *thirteen* years ago
And the present at the carnival
I *had* to go find out
You had been a dream for too long

47

I decided to finish my waffle
Approach the rubbish bin
That the man was standing next to
And flow from there
I looked down to eat my last bite
When I looked up
To take that loooong awaited step
To *him*
To possibly...you!
He was gone
People everywhere
No clue of a direction to go
He just...disappeared
And a moment flashed again
Wondering
If you really are an angel
A story in my head
A dream

*

After that things changed
I fell into a limbo world
I had stepped out of
The one I was living
But missed the one I went for
I was *walking* to *you*
Only a moment too late
I tried to reconcile—that that was it
My chance had passed
I thought perhaps
It was my karma
For walking away from you

I felt like I emotionally cheated on Dante
And told him of the experience
When I returned to New York
He *excitedly* asked if I went up to you

I said I hesitated
Because I wanted to be respectful to our life
But decided I had to know
Then waited a moment too long
Dante assured me if it was you
And I did want to be with you
And you with I
That he understood
I told him I wished I knew that before

"Well, how would you feel
If the situation was reversed?"
He asked.

"Of *course* I would want you to be happy,"
I replied .

"Well then, there you go," he said.

A new lesson of relationship:
I love you and you are free

*

After that
I felt the relationship changing
We both dove
Into our respective artistic endeavors
We saw how much enjoyment
The other was having
And made space for it

But between my job
And going to Amsterdam
It left little time for relationship
My books, Dante's art
Were the children of our union
That we nurtured for one another

With our shared love of art
We were each other's sounding board
For different ideas
We went after dreams
That brought us bliss
And lived the NYC life
Trying to get our art out
It was a special connection
Because we began them at the same time
We could celebrate each other's successes
And empathize the rejections

Dante and I were both on fire
He'd do exhibits
I would do book parties
Of which I'd pick a charity to support

*

Life went very fast from there
My injury became another nuisance
Learning how to heal and manage pain
Became like going back to school
It affected our relationship
I struggled with depression
Being off work
Going back
Getting retriggered
Taking work leaves again
The cycle got old very quickly

The injury became my whole focus
Trying different techniques
Asking doctors endless questions
I learned a lot about the body, the mind
And pain
It took a few years to get there
But when I did

I appreciated the injury's silver lining
I had learned so much
And felt stronger for it
Even healthier
But in those years
The relationship suffered

*

2016
Well
That's when the crumbling
Of lives began
With a lot of loss
My health suffered after that year
Mental and emotional fatigue
Watching my father die
From his diagnoses in January
To his death in December

Mike was my first text
When I sat on the plane at LaGuardia
To fly to Michigan
The morning my father died
As soon as I landed
And turned on my phone
It rang
It was Mike
Knowing him he probably redialed
Until it connected
Knowing us
We were connected in that way
And his voice grounded me
Into the experience I was embarking
Of burying my father

The physical fatigue affected my injury
I was miserable

Head, heart, and body all in pain
I pushed Dante away
And ended our relationship
Then slowly, at first
Began to slip under
The surface of life

At the end of 2016
My future self appeared
And was very direct

"Look," he said.
"First, let's acknowledge
This is a lot of loss and change at once
It may feel really intense at times
And perhaps for awhile
But remember eighteen years ago
Joe
Coming out
Those were a few rough years
It *was* a lot for someone your age
And at times you didn't think
You were going to make it through
Didn't want to
But
You *did!*

And remember?
Right afterward when you left London?
And rose from the ashes
Remember how *bright* & *exciting* life felt?
How in love with life you were?
And it was that bright love for life
That brought you Angel
Because that is what you put out
That is who you are
Love
Remember that

Now
Let it sear in your heart

There may be times
In the coming years
As you wade through this
That you don't think you will make it
But you *will!*
Remember how wonderful it will feel
On the other side of this
No matter *how* dark it gets
Remember!!
It will be equally as bright
After the darkest night!
I'll be waiting there on the other side
To celebrate with you
Don't forget
Stay strong
You got this!

*

Future Anthony returned to the future
Present Anthony began mourning
Trying to heal
It was up
Then down
Then up again
But healing was the priority

I discovered a beautiful community
Of people with Modo yoga
After everything I tried
Their sequence of postures
Targeted exactly what my body needed
It was tremendously helpful
In managing my injury
I loved it so much

I got trained to teach
Learned more about the body
Creatied an even healthier routine
Then before the accident

I continued working on the third book
Knowing the writing brought
Both pleasure and healing
As it challenged me creatively
I kept getting ideas and tinkered with it
A little here
A little there
When I could
But there wasn't a lot of time

*

Progress in healing
And maintaining a healthy routine
Took a big setback
When my base in New York was closed
I began commuting to L.A. for work
My home was the last stable thing I had
I didn't want to change that too
Even though I was gone
Up to three weeks at a time
Month after month
The fatigue drained me
Compounded and made me miserable
Amplifying the pain
And getting retriggered
The merry-go-round
Was anything but merry
Faster and faster it spun
I didn't know how to get off
How to *literally* stop moving
Hotel after hotel
Rarely in my own bed

Had me so ungrounded

*

What can I say?
At a certain point
When it doesn't feel like it's letting up
You struggle to keep
Your head above water
You let go and go under
And wait to come back up
Wonder if you will
If you want to

I dropped into a deep depression
Thoughts of suicide entered
Life didn't seem worth it
The dual consciousness began
The part of me that wanted to try
The part of me that didn't

*

Every hotel room I entered
I climbed into bed
Usually for the entire layover
I avoided invites from co-workers
I was a 'slam clicker' as we say in the industry
The door was slammed
And the lock was clicked
The only reasons I left the bed
Were for food or the bathroom
Until the next flight
The curtains would get drawn
To shut out the world
Especially when the sun was shining
That really annoyed me
I felt less guilty wasting my time on Earth

When it was gloomy out
And I matched the weather
I slept or zoned out on TV
To conserve energy for the next day's façade
The façade to myself as well
That everything was ok
Until one day
Some day in the future
When it's not
And everything begins
Crumbling down

*

I had begun taking anti-depressants
After my father's death
Then stopped after five months
When they seemed
To have served their purpose
And I felt better

Now a year later
Seven months into the commute
In a hotel room in San Francisco
The part of me that wanted to give up
Wanted to be heard
Wanted a voice
And in that moment was given one

"I want to die," I said.

I needed to feel the vibrations
Of *those* words out of *my* mouth
And validate the part of me
That meant them
Really meant them
The part of me that wanted to fight
Was chilled to hear the words

Yet acknowledged them
Then reached for the anti-depressants
I kept in my travel bag
Doubled the dose I had taken before
And into my mouth they were thrown

But the thoughts of suicide persisted
Became constant
At times I was aware and questioned
'Why am I still thinking about suicide
So much?'

A kindred spirit popped into my head
Ms. Gloria Vanderbilt—
And an interview I remember seeing
She spoke to her son Carter
Not being suicidal & was adamant
That the anti-depression medication
Produced the thoughts
It was the first time
I'd heard such a theory
And it stuck in my sub-conscious
Because it seemed like such an oxymoron

*

My awareness became in-tuned
To anti-depressants commercials
Popping up
In hotel room after hotel room
They advised to see a doctor
If thoughts of suicide began
Then Gloria popped in my head again
And dots connected
The ads weren't for the medication I was on
But in the foggy confusion
Of my depression
At times clarity came through

Perhaps specific to my brain chemistry
And the particular one I was on
They produced the thoughts in me
Or amplified the ones
That were already there

After a few months
Sticking up for the conditioned thoughts
That their purpose
Is to help me feel *better*
And had before
Yet taking into account
The thoughts of death that persisted
The part of me that wanted to try
And stay on Earth
Got really scared
And I immediately went off them

*

When Phillip Seymour Hoffman died
After fourteen years sobriety
I was shocked
Both because I had no idea
He had used drugs in the past
And because it made me wonder
What happened??
To make him go back
After such a long time?
At the time I was around six years
Sans crystal meth—
Ugh, that's the one for me
That makes me so uncomfortable to say —
Like Voldemort—
And to associate it with me
Because the after affects
Mentally, emotionally, and physically
Were the most difficult to deal with

At the time Phillip died
Dante and I were doing fine
I had *no* desire *whatsoever*
Alcohol was never my thing
Yes, pot and mushrooms from time to time
But I was usually in a good space
I won't say I'd never do those again
But hard drugs didn't interest me at the time
But hearing Phillip's story was *so* humbling
He must have had a perfect storm
After *fourteen* years
And from that point on
I had a deeper respect
For the time I had
Of not using crystal meth
Along with the awareness
That life can throw you off
At any moment

*

For me the storm was brewing
For several years
After dealing with my father dying
And my relationship ending
An injury coupled with a dehumanizing
David and Goliath battle
With an insurance company for years
Lawyers, court dates, fighting
For the rights of my health
The commute that had me home
No more than a week
For the eleventh month straight
Suicidal thoughts for months
In addition to the hatred
Coming from the administration
As they attempted to strip
Hard-fought LGBTQIA rights

Human rights
That shouldn't have had to be fought for
In the first place
The politics in this country
Were more than abusive
The hateful rhetoric
Coming out of their mouths
Was dehumanizing
And blaringly amplified on a national stage
Blatantly disrespectful
Flashback feelings
Of the difficulty in coming out
And the various homophobic experiences
From years before and since in my life
In friends' lives
In brothers' and sisters' lives I never met
But having heard their stories
Having felt their pain
Continued triggering
The trauma of that period

*

The subtle
Homophobic
Thoughts, actions, and requests
That bubbled to the surface within family
The clarity of recognizing them intellectually
As homophobia came through to me
The unconscious feelings
That felt irksome over previous years
Feelings of being less than equal
To my brothers flooded back
And reminded me of the person
I was taught to hate long ago
Nearly twenty years prior
All over again
My rational brain tried to tell myself

It is the societal and religious conditioning
Of the times they grew up in
It's *not* how they really feel
It *can't* be

No, I was not the teenager
Kicked out of their home for being gay
Like at the Ali Forney Center
But however far the other side
Of the spectrum
A homophobic response may seem
However slight to someone else
When the slightest trigger is presented
It is the original experience
Of all the hurt
The feelings of self-hate and self-disgust
That take one right back
To the original traumatic moments
That's PTSD

*

I could no longer stuff it all down
To keep calm and carry on
All the anger and sadness
Of so much being triggered...

It made me want to escape *that* person—
To escape myself—
Turning my storm
Perfect
And somewhere in the weeks
Before I went off the anti-depressants
For the first time in nine years
Voldemort and I
Met again

*

I was so lonely for intimacy...to be touched
I jumped online and met a guy
I didn't expect Voldemort to be there
But when he appeared
There was no hesitation

'What the *fuck* just happened!'
I thought the next morning walking home
It was like a bomb went off in my life
I was in shock

'That will *never* happen again!'

But the next time I was in town
I reached out to the same man
Never thinking there would be drugs...
Again
He didn't have any & asked if I did
"*No*," I said.
He had a friend in Brooklyn
And asked if I wanted to go
No
I didn't!
But he was sweet too
And I *did want* intimacy
I didn't want to start over
With someone new

*

I met him in the East Village
And we jumped into a cab
As we rode to Brooklyn
We got to know each other a little better
I was sharing about my job
And the New York base closing
How I had been commuting to Los Angeles
For the last eleven months

How it was taking its toll on me
As soon as I paused
He spoke in a tone
Like he went
Somewhere

"I was at gate eleven
When the bomb went off at gate twelve
During the terrorist attack
At Brussels Airport."
An *enormous* record scratch
Went off in my mind
It was such an unexpected thing to hear
In a cab in Manhattan
On our way to do drugs in Brooklyn
Like a bomb going off
Again
Through a story
Of an *actual* bomb
Going off
I froze for a second as it registered

"*WHAT?*
You were *standing*
Next to a *bomb*
When it went off?"

I repeated the words
Not believing what I heard
And needed to hear it
With my question
I didn't know what else to say
I had already said enough
Just by *saying* the word...eleven

Which was a trigger for him...
A *word*
He continued to tell bits of the story

I just tried—
Being sober at the time—
To listen
Absorb

Allow him to share what he wanted to share
Which included climbing over rubble
Past dead bodies with their faces
And/or limbs blown off
Just to get out alive

"My god.
I'm *so* sorry you experienced that."
It was all I could think of to say
Before the subject gradually changed
Then, we arrived in Brooklyn
Where both of our storms were escaped
Temporarily, with drugs

Not long after we arrived
He wanted to leave
In my now high-mind
We *just* got there
I asked if he minded if I stayed
Said he didn't
So I did
As the night stretched into morning
The thought that came with it…

'Why did I do this *again?'*

Nine years now twice within a month
The shame was doubled

*

The Anthony that returned after sobering up
Realized what the man told me
Only hours before

Even though I didn't have
A full understanding of PTSD at that time
The good in me judged myself

'How could I have done that?!'

Even though he was still
Essentially a stranger
How could I have let him go home
Alone
After what he shared with me

I hated that aspect of drugs
The selfish side
That made me think of myself
Thank god he left his glasses

"I'll bring them back to him," I said.

I jumped at the chance

He came over to my home the next night
His demeanor was more shy and reserved
Not on drugs
We lied in bed
He on his back
As I placed my arm across his chest
With the rest of my body half on top of his
And my cheek on the pillow
Safely
Snuggled close to his
I wanted to apologize
But the words wouldn't come
Instead

"Do you mind if I ask you
What the terrorist attack was like?
I'd understand

If you don't want to talk about it."

But he simply began
Like the play button was pushed
And he was back
Narrating while reliving
And staring at the ceiling
Not a flinch in his monotone voice
He was back in Brussels airport
The experience so present
That I merged in
Lying so close
Safely in my bed
As I closed my eyes
And went to Brussels with him

"My mother was driving me to the airport,"
He began. "I was flying back to New York."

From there he spared no detail
Every pristine and clear second
And through a portal I was there
I could *see* it
I could *feel* it through his words
With each horrific part
My body reacted
Instinctively cringed
Squeezed and clutched to his
As if for safety
Absorbing where the shrapnel
Entered his body
The second bomb going off
The ceiling falling down
On to the ground
On to people
The screams of the people
Running into a small airline office for cover
About twenty-five people crammed

And locked into a small room
Crying and screaming inside the room
Outside the room
As gunshots rapidly fired
Just outside the door
More people dying in real time
Just outside the door
After about thirty minutes
A knock

"It was the Belgian army," he said.

"Oh good
You were being saved," I replied.

"Yes, but at that moment
We didn't know the army had arrived
We thought it was the terrorists
Coming to kill us
We were trapped
There were no windows
And only one door
Everyone started to scream."

I cringed and squeezed him again
Trying to imagine
The *horrific* sound
Of cacophonic screams
From people trapped together
Believing they were about to die
What the *vibration* of *that*
Must have felt like
Piercing into their consciousness
Into their subconscious
Into the cells of their body

"My god I can't imagine," I said.
"Less than an hour prior

Safely with your *mother*
About to fly to New York
Now the *Belgian army, bombs*, and *gunfire*
Are part of your life experience," I said .

He continued

Once the army
Led them out of the room
They were instructed to climb over
The mound of rubble
That was less than an hour ago…the *ceiling*
Which now blocked the only way out
While the soldiers covered them
From the terrorists' bullets
Still flying through the air

Just before he started climbing
He looked to his right and saw a mother
With two young children
And a third in a stroller
The woman just looked at him
Without any words
Her expression screaming it all
'Help!'
He scooped the older children up
One underneath each arm
Like a roll of carpet
And began climbing
Navigating around dead bodies
With no faces or limbs
Up the rubble
Then back down and out of the airport
Where ambulances awaited
And he gave the children
Back to the mother
"So you're a hero," I said.

He didn't say anything to that
Brushed it off
Like the title didn't matter to him
One he'd prefer not to have

"Then I just walked
Past paramedics and police
They tried to stop me
To see if I was alright
I didn't stop
Or say anything
I wanted to get to the field
That stretches into the distance
From the airport."

"Why?" I asked confused.
"Didn't you want help or to get
Checked out by medical professionals?"

"I knew my mother
Would hear the news on the radio
Turn around and come back," he said.
"I needed to get to the one road
That led to the airport
To my mother
So I just kept walking."

The road was jammed with cars
Of people trying to get back
To their loved ones
Stalled with thoughts
Whether they were alive or dead

Once he got to the road
He walked past each car
Looking, searching for his mother's vehicle
Finally in the distance
He saw her

And she him
She jumped out of the car
And started running toward him

"Full circle back to your mother
All of that happening in what
Just over an hour?" I asked.

"Yes," he said.
"And the funny thing is
My mother has a disease
She's handicap
And if affects her walking
I've *never* seen her run like that."

"Wow!" I replied.
"A mother's love."

*

When he finished his story
And we were both back from Brussels
In my Chelsea bed, 2018
We had sex
Afterward he looked at me
With a bit of a bewildered look

"Wow," he began.
"Sex without drugs."

'*Yes,* of course,' I thought.
'Sex without drugs.'

But I didn't say it
I certainly was not going to judge him
For doing drugs
Not after hearing his story
But I sure began judging myself

*

Since my suicidal thoughts had begun
It was as if my spirit
Dropped down to the River Styx
Paced back and forth along its banks
Pondering
Whether to whistle for the ferryman Charon
To bring me over
Now it seemed I was meeting others
Along its banks as well

*

Why didn't I reach out for help?
Because of the biological reaction called
Shame
It's a nasty one
The parts of myself
I wanted to reject
Eject right out of me
Were torturing, infecting, and controlling
So much of what I did
I was ashamed to talk about it
Because of fear
That no one would believe me

*

Growing up in the "toughen up"
Cultural mentality
As the phrases
"Be a man"
"Suck it up"
"Be strong"
Replayed in my head
It makes me sick to admit it
But I was emotionally invalidating myself

As though my feelings didn't matter
And were wrong to experience
It was destructive and unkind
But I couldn't help it

*

Also, I feared I would be shunned
Because suicide is such a heavy subject
People don't know how to handle it
How to respond
Or they don't say anything
After making yourself so vulnerable
That you open up to the wrong person
And their reaction or non-action
Sends you into further despair
That they'll think you're fucked up
Or *crazy*
Man I *hate* that word
For people that deal with mental illness
It's as bad as faggot to a gay person
In my opinion
Or that I'd be called dramatic
An addict
A lost cause
Or all the other labels
I projected
That someone might give me
It would be like coming out again
To share such darkness

And until
I stopped pushing those parts
Of myself away
And rather weaved them back in
Through self-acceptance
And compassion
To become capable of loving *all* of myself

Until I didn't care what anyone thought
Because I knew the stigma was an illusion
Because I wanted to be happy
The secret got a lid put on it
As it festered and began
To slowly come to a boil
A *perfect* storm brewing
Releasing the lid occasionally
By doing drugs
Making everything feel like chaos
In my internal world
Out of control
Yet fooling myself I had control
Because I was able
To be highly functioning
By showing up to work
Yet, it is the "highly functioning"
That can hide how much
They actually struggle

*

I thought to call Mike
The last time we spoke was in the spring
We had a long catch up
A *great* talk
When I returned
From a month in Nicaragua
After my yoga training
Wow I felt great!
Vegan diet, no sugar, caffeine, or pot
Yoga two, three, four times a day
Eight, nine hours of sound sleep
Every night
Living in the jungle
Surrounded by nature
And beautiful, positive people
I literally felt like I had aged backwards

Ten years
With the energy and mobility
That came with it

I was excited to share with Mike
My next plan
Mike was always curious
Showed genuine interest
In where my head was at
What I was planning next
If New York was my final destination

"I know it's like winning the lottery
To support myself with my writing, Mike
But I like it
And I still want to live in Amsterdam."

My next plan to get there was via yoga
Teach for a couple years at Modo NYC
Before I could put in a request
For a franchise studio in Amsterdam
And continue the writing on the side

"If it's what you enjoy
And what you want to do
Then do it," he encouraged.
"But come to Chicago for a visit soon.
When was the last time you were here?
When was the last time you saw Ben
And we were all together?"

"I don't even remember," I replied.

"I think it was that New Year's Eve
When we all went to that house party
With Stephanie."

"Yeah I think you're right.

That was a lot of fun."

"It was."
"Come on! Come to Chicago
That was sooo long ago."

"I know, I *know*…I will."

*

Months later
With a fall from yoga grace
I wanted to reach out
But didn't

'I'm always turning to Mike with heavy stuff.
I'll call when I pull myself out of this
And I'm better.'

I knew of *all* people
There was no hiding it from—
It was Mike
Except by not calling
A memory from Chicago resurfaced—
I hadn't come out yet
And had stayed out all night
When I came back to his place in the morning
Mike asked, "Did you do any drugs?"

"Yes," I replied.

"What?"

There was no reason to lie to him
I felt his love
"Crystal."

"You know how bad that is for you, right?"

"I know...I know."

And it was left at that
There was no judgment
No interference in my free will
A gentle alert

"Alright, let's go get some deep dish
I have a craving
You must be starving."

"Yeah, I could eat."

*

Now
All these years later
At middle-age
And a tumble down that road again
I didn't believe
It would be so easy
For him to overlook it
It was all projection
Because I was having a hard time
Overlooking it myself

*

Not long after the Belgian-hero experience
I was heading to Amsterdam
For another writing period
That would help
To get away
From the pressure cooker
I felt Manhattan becoming
But no sooner was I there
When I went on a date
Drugs came up again

'Geez,' I thought.
'Doesn't *anybody*
Have sex without drugs?'

I had been isolated in relationship
I had no idea
How prevalent hard drugs were
No judgment of course!
In a good headspace, healthy dosage
And a safe environment
Not harming yourself or anyone else
To connect, enhance
Or expand your consciousness
Let some stress out
Do your thing
Live your life

But that wasn't true for me at the time
And a day or two after that episode
When the vomiting and diarrhea arrived
Something certainly was not right
I had *never* felt like that before
I could barely stand or walk
As I made my way through Oosterpark
To OLVG hospital
It felt like I'd never get there
Each tiny step I took
Resting along the way
The shame forcing me to conceal
That something was wrong with me
From strangers passing by
As I tried to walk as "normal" as possible

I had never been to a Dutch hospital
A new spot that *you* could have been
I did wonder sometimes
What you might have chosen as a career
Once I saw a T.V. host that looked like you

And wondered *perhaps*
An actor or newscaster
Then paid attention
Whenever I watched Dutch television

A doctor or nurse
Had also crossed my mind
Not that I wanted a reason
To go to the hospital to find out
But now I had one
And if you were a doctor
I certainly did not want to run into you
In my current state
And for the reason that brought me
But you weren't there either
What I thought might be food poisoning
Sounded more like some bacterial infection
I think they said
The only thing I comprehended
Was that I had to let it
Work out of my system

Well
That took three weeks
I've never been so sick
I've never stayed in bed so long
I've never had to use the toilet so much
Persistent diarrhea
The two-minute walk to Albert Heijn
Was like trekking
Through a Siberian Tundra for supplies
I didn't know how to take care of myself
Or what I needed
Nor was I able to realize
That the diarrhea was dehydrating me
Making me so weak
I was afraid to eat anything
It just came right back out

I lived on applesauce
Thank god Art was in Scotland
And I had the place to myself
I was too ashamed
To reach out to anyone for help
To bring me supplies
Too ashamed to admit the reason
Why I was so sick
And made the decision
To just let it work out of my system
'This is a perfect reason to stop drugs,'
I thought after returning to New York
My writing period ruined

*

As Thanksgiving approached
I went to the Hamptons
To stay at my friend Liza's cottage
To regroup in nature
Reset and breathe
Liza insisted
I come to her family dinner
I resisted
Thanksgiving
Was the last time I saw my father
Before he died three weeks later
And I ended my relationship
I insisted on being alone
Manhattan began to feel
Like a dark lair beneath the water
Where I dove back under again
With another episode
A couple days before Christmas
Then back to The Hamptons
The next day
Again Liza insisted I be with her family
Again I resisted

But instead of leaving me alone
She left her dog Lilly
To keep me company

Along with 1980's
George and Whitney
I played their music over and over
Singing and dancing with Lilly
Around Liza's tree
It brought me back to childhood
A more innocent time
Mixed in with holiday
Also a kindred time of connection
Bonding empethetically to the artists
They knew
What it was like to struggle
With substance abuse
But they were good people too
And gave a lot
I tried to remind myself
I was a good person too
Who gave a lot

I attempted to raise my vibration
Through positivity
Through the therapy
Of music, singing, dancing, nature...
And Lilly
A fresh start
To leave that behavior
And those choices in 2018

*

It lasted only a week
As 2019 started with another episode
But a couple days later things changed
After six months

Of an intimate relationship
With suicidal thoughts
Kept alone inside my head
I reached out for help

On New Year's Day Dante received word
A friend attempted suicide
The next day
Another friend's family member
Did commit suicide
It hit too close
One attempt and one death

A couple days later
I walked one block to Callen Lourde
To speak to someone
About the thoughts in my head
I confided in Dante that night
And Liza a few days later
Liza led me to my therapist
The first session I got lost in thinking
Before saying

"Six months, that's kind of a long time
To think about suicide, huh?"

"Ahhh, yeah!"
She said with raised eyebrows
And wide eyes
Her expression and delivery
Were perfect
And broke the heaviness of the subject
It was received with the humor
I felt she intended
I laughed
A little humor interjected
When speaking of darkness
Goes a long way

64

I knew I found the right therapist

But I did not tell *any* of them
About the drug use
Just the suicidal thoughts
I felt I could hide it from them
Which is why I chose them
Instead of Mike

'I'll touch base with him soon
When I'm better…I'm getting there,'
I thought.

But
There were more episodes in the New Year
Both sides of the pond
Then a couple months without
I tried to be conscious
Of the time between each
And it did get longer
But then a few more in the spring
Around Mike and my birthdays
We texted as we usually did
But no catch up by phone
There was a fraternity reunion that autumn
I wanted to know if he was going
I had no desire to
And would only go if he was
But he didn't plan on it

*

For the second half of 2019
There was no visit with Voldemort
For six months!
I began to see light
At the end of the tunnel
I remembered how much lighter it would feel

I came up with a new plan
To move to Amsterdam
Permanently
I no longer wanted to wait two years
To teach yoga in New York
Before I could apply for a franchise
Life was too short

With Art's encouragement
We talked of starting a business
Ideas percolated to *just do it*
I was happy with the decision
Since the country was not going
In a great direction for me
Plus, battling against people's opinions
That it wasn't patriotic to abandon ship
Made me want to ex-pat more
Are you kidding me?
Actions speak louder than words
"All men are created equal"
Words I heard all my life
Are you fucking kidding me?
It's like telling your friend
Whose husband
Repeatedly beats him
To stick it out, give it another try
No
Walk in my shoes for a second
Or any other minority
It was time to leave
The *abusive*-consciousness relationship
I felt in America

*

And momentum began
To create a new chapter
Even into 2020

I was getting a better handle on life
Feeling healthier in mind, body, and spirit
Rising up
To start again
In Amsterdam!
I was going on month six without drugs
When I went to Michigan
To visit my mother for the holidays
I thought of Mike when I landed in Chicago
I was trying to figure out
If I could fit a quick drop in
Maybe on the way back?

The next morning I woke
To a What's App message from him
"Yo son," he wrote.
I laughed
That's so Mike
"Hey how are you?
I was thinking of you the other day
When I passed through Chicago
On my way to Grand Rapids
And that it's been too long."
As the busyness of the holidays began
Neither of us followed up

*

I made a last minute decision
To go to Brazil at the end of 2019
I needed a new continent, a new culture
And their perspective energetically
Philosophically
And literally from *their* spot on Earth
To start a new decade

I was in New York Christmas day
And the lonely feeling that came

With being alone
Led to a visit with Voldemort
The six-month streak broken
But it was the longest since it began
Just over a year prior
Progress, I positively felt—
As I let up on the self-criticism—
Was the perspective I tried to take

*

In Ipanema
While walking the promenade
On my way
To Copacabana Beach for the fireworks—
Wow!
Rio knows how to do New Year's
Best fireworks *ever*!—
I thought to reach out to Mike
We spent many New Year's Eves
Or around that time
Together over the years
But the shame
Of a too recent visit with Voldemort
Stopped me
'After Brazil...yes
We *will* connect
I'll be honest about all the darkness
He will be ok with it
Supportive
It's *Mike!*
I'm *sure* of it
Plus I'll have some amazing adventures
To share from Brazil
Balance out the heaviness
Make up for it,' I thought.

Upon my return to New York

I checked my flying schedule for February
I received a Chicago layover
I bid for to see Mike

'Perfect! I'll surprise him!'

*

Cue:
A global pandemic?

My schedule had me flying
The last two weeks of February
The Chicago trip was at the end
Afterward
I was going to Michigan
For a couple of weeks
To help my mother
Before and after a surgery

As the anxiety of the world
And the passengers—
More and more wearing masks
With each flight—
Began percolating
It seeped into my consciousness
Wondering
What is this?
What *is* happening?
Hearing the first death in America
Announced from the television set
Of my San Jose hotel room
Now
It
Was happening here

I hadn't contacted Mike
About the trip to Chicago

I wanted to surprise him
But as the two weeks went on
Flying back to back trips
Fatigue set in
Worry set in
About getting the virus
With all the places and all the people
I was coming into contact with
And bringing it to my mother
With a soon-to-be
Even more compromised immune system
After her surgery

Worry
That with her age and anesthesia
There's a chance
She could die during the surgery
So I made the decision at the last minute
To cancel Chicago
Then, I'd have five days with her
Instead of three before the surgery

'I'll catch up with Mike
When I get back to New York'

*

As my mother and I watched
The pandemic unfold from the television
Cases gradually increasing
And spreading in New York
I made arrangements to get back

"Why don't you just stay here?"
My mother suggested.

I thought about it
But I was exhausted and ungrounded

Being away from home for a month
I had some doctor's appointments
An epidural for my injury
A crown that needed to be cast
And was wary of an approaching shutdown
Of *everything*

"It's getting bad in New York," she said.
You're going into the eye of the storm."

But that was *my* home
And I wanted to go home
Which I did
The day before everything locked down
Except for essentials
I needed to take care of myself now
It was good to be home

And as frustrating
As it was appearing to be
It looked like
I would be home in New York
Longer than expected
My plan to be in Amsterdam
Continually being altered by the pandemic
Still unaware
What lurked in the near future
So close!
Finally going after my dream…again
Never would I have imagined
There would be a day
When I wasn't even *allowed*
In Amsterdam

So, instead of leaving New York
I am here on this day
The 16th of September 2020

Part III

Anthony is writing
In his apartment
Many months after
He passed Angel on the street.

This is what I would have asked you
Had I turned around:
"Are you are indeed
The love of my life?"

*

Why?
Why didn't I turn around?
Go back
And just see?

I did wonder
If it was you as we passed
Doubt crept in
Disbelief

'There's a pandemic going on
Foreigners aren't allowed in the country,'
My head said.

'What if he is flight crew?
Or an essential worker?'
My heart replied.

And so again
Like all the other sightings
I did a second look
To see you standing
In the spot where we passed
I wondered why
'Is he looking at a text?
Or something else?'
I turned my head forward
And began to cross the street

'Maybe he has been living in Manhattan
All along!'

Screamed my heart.
'You're planning a *move* to Amsterdam!
Part of the reason
Is that you hope
To run into him there
What if he came here first?
And is living here!
Do a second look!
Do a second look!'
My heart *pleaded.*

I began to turn my head
To do a second look
And that is when
A 'Beauty and the Beast' moment
Erupted
You, Beauty of course
The beast in me reflected
With flashbacks by demons
I wanted to reject
In a matter of seconds
Trapping me on either side
With images of someone
I thought I was
Whom I didn't like
Who hadn't been very nice to me
In recent months
Who had been…a beast
In that relationship with myself
That served as my reference
I thought I would hurt you too
And of *all* the people on the planet
I would not want to hurt
That would be *you*

*

If you've ever had flashbacks from PTSD

Wohhhh
It's a time warping, jarring experience
The brain is unable to distinguish
The flashback from the past
And re-experiences it
All over again
The rush of emotion
And fight or flight response
Soars the adrenalin

One flashback:
All the mistakes I made in relationship
Collaged into an image of a beast

I hadn't processed
My relationship with Dante
Because we were still connected
Sharing the home until the pandemic
The logical aspects, yes
We weren't having sex
Or spending time with the other's family
Seeing a lot less of one another too
Overlapping sometimes
But the *us*
That was just Dante and Anthony
The mental and emotional aspect
The reflecting, healing, and growing
From the experience
Was not dealt with
Because it was still happening
In a different way
We were not together
But not completely separated either
Learning lessons from relationship
Weren't priority
My father and health came first
Those took awhile

I still needed Dante
I understood I was breaking a heart
And to ask that we evolve
Instantly to friendship was a lot
But I was desperate that we did
I needed help with daily activities
Groceries, errands
Keeping my appointments
For head, heart, and body
These were my focus
Working out again began
With two-pound weights
I couldn't believe it
But Dante was there
A solider of love

*

But eventually the day would come
When they would need to be addressed
And it did
Two weeks before
We passed on the street
Dante had met someone
And was moving out

The shelved, emotional aspects
Of our relationship
Came tumbling down
Of course the beast in me at the time
Beat myself up first
For the mistakes I made
The times I could have been a little more
Ok, a lot more mature

I was flooded
With all the *good* Dante had done
All the love he gave

71

I was randomly crying a lot
In the two weeks prior to seeing you
But with Dante's help
The tide turned quickly
In a few weeks
I was on the other side
Of healing the 'us' of our past
Along with solidifying
The friendship we established

Dante recalled all the good I did
The gifts I brought
The love I gave
He also reminded me
He wasn't a saint all the time either
And he wasn't...wink

But I wasn't there yet
With your appearance
On my street that day

*

The day Dante told me he was moving out
He asked
Why *did* I break up with him?
In that moment it dawned on me
I had no idea
Everything fell apart so fast that year
When I reflected I realized
I lost all self-love
I was shocked
'How did that happen?' I thought.
And more importantly
'How do I get it back?'
It had been nearly twenty years
Since meeting you
That I learned self-love

By coming out
Never did I consider
That once you found self-love
You could lose it

*

It reminds me of a time
When I took unconditional self-love
For granted
Years before, Dante and I were driving
I was singing along to the music
Just being silly and playful
And he asked
"How do you love yourself so much?"
I thought he was joking
But when I realized he was really asking
I pondered it for a moment
I replied I hated myself for so long
Taught to hate myself
By the religion and culture
I grew up in
And I had *a lot* of making up to do!

Now it seemed
I was *right* back
Where I started
It broke my heart

*

What was the second flashback?
My naked dead body
Overdosed on a bed in June
What was I doing dead on a bed?
Let's go back to the first week of April
As the pandemic began hitting New York
And the number of deaths began
Its exponentially steep climb

*

While inside most of the day
I was getting so much done
Administration and deep cleaning—
Getting rid of *junk*—
All the stuff that piles up for years
And I had been dying to do…
Forever

Then, I wanted to start making phone calls
To *all* those people
Who for months, and some years
I had wanted to properly catch up with
And now, check in on
During the new universal experience
Of a global *pandemic*
To properly catch up with… Mike
I called him on a Monday
It went to voicemail

"Mike! How are you?
Hope this finds you doing well
And *safe*
In these crazy times!
Call me! It's been way too long!"

A couple days passed
I felt insecure
'Had I let too much time pass
Since we chatted?
No, I told myself
Don't be silly
I'm someone he always wants in his life
He said so himself
The night he pulled me
Out of the closet.'

Another day passed
'Come on Mike!
I know life gets busy
But I *really* miss you!'

That evening
I received an email from our friend Ben
Whom I had not been in touch with for years
Even before I read the words
I knew
Mike was dead

My best friend who walked
Through so much darkness with me

My friend who
Because of him
I met you in the dark
Gone
Suddenly
And young

*

My future self
Made another emergency appearance
Reminding me that I survived
The losses of Joe and Mohammad
I tried to embrace that
I *really* did
Be strong in that knowing
Of those experiences

But with Joe I had Mike
With Mohammad I had Dante
Now, being single
I was alone
And forced to be in lockdown

73

With the demons
Mike's death was conjuring
The lack of social support—
Because the entire world
Was in mandatory lockdown—
Plus the ongoing stress and depression
From the previous few years
Made me a member
Of the mental illness pandemic
The Covid-19 pandemic spawned

No travels to defibrillate the soul
Like I had through mourning Joe

No lover to lie next to
Like I had when mourning Mohammad

*

I *really* made an effort
To *celebrate* Mike
And I did in that first month
I listened and danced to tracks
I knew he would love
Mike would get so excited about new music
That he loved and wanted to share
He introduced me to so much

I laughed out loud at memories of him
A sommelier of humor
Proven by the fact
That the same hearty laugh
He produced from me the first time
Could be replicated in intensity
Years later
And if you made Mike laugh
It was like receiving your PhD in comedy
He had great respect for good humor

Mike was fun to explore with
Wherever the day took us
His carefree curiosity
Of trying this or that
Going here or there
Was easy to be with and infectious
If he liked a particular song, film, or food
I wanted to hear it, see it, taste it

Yes, of course there was sadness
That first month too
But it was still so surreal
No funeral
No gathering
It hadn't sunk in
And someone like Mike
Had to be celebrated first

*

I also had a very unexpected
Yet extremely special sprite pop in
The first lighthouse flash—
Or rather rainbow flash—
In the form of a Rainbow Fairy
A pint size cameo
But boy!
She nailed it!

The day after the news of Mike
A rainbow appeared in the window
Of the townhouse
Across from mine
I was confused at first
Because it faced me
I tried to make out
If I was just seeing through
The back of the white paper

But no
It was purposely facing my building
It was such sweet innocence
It soothed my soul
Every time I looked at it
And was a moment of peace in my heart
Several weeks it stayed up there
And her beautiful magic
Continued within that first month

One day
A commercial came on for orphaned dogs
It began with a song:

Ohhhh, why you look so sad?
Tears are in your eyes
Come on and come to me now
Don't
Be ashamed to cry
Let me see you through
'Cause I've seen the dark side too...

And boom
The tears *were* in my eyes
Because Mike saw me through
Saw the dark side too
He stood by me

I YouTubed the song
And listened to it in full
The words were Mike
Coming to me in that moment
Its title led my thoughts to the film
Stand By Me
The feeling of the friendship
Between the boys in that film
Encapsulated the essence
Of how I felt about my friendship with Mike

That inner adolescence
On an adventure together
With all the ups and downs
Dealing with life's bullies and mishaps
Taking risks for adrenaline rushes
Simply having each others' backs
Exploring through life's forests—
Or Red Light Districts—
Together
I listened to 'Stand By Me' next
Trying to find comfort in those facts

Not long after
As spring was blooming
With my window open
I heard music playing
Then singing
It was Rainbow Fairy
Floating around her garden
Singing!
'Stand by Me'
Ohhhh how she belted out
"So darlin' darlin'
Stand by me
Ohhhh
Stand by me!"

My heart both melted and smiled
As I lied on my bed and listened
To the precious
Beautiful
Absolutely *magical*
Rainbow Fairy

*

But as Mike's birthday approached in May
The reality sunk in more

I wouldn't reach out to him
And he to me the following week
Our birthdays six days apart

I wanted to just *be* with somebody
I wanted intimacy
To be *touched*
Held
After no funeral
No hugs
No contact from anyone of any kind

Yes, I was lonely
Perhaps I looked in the wrong place
I got on Scruff
And found someone
I didn't go looking for drugs
But when drugs presented themselves
Again, I didn't say no

My streak of nearly five months
Broken
And the slippery slope you hear about
When doing drugs to escape
Rather than to connect
Fuuuuuuck
It's an easy slide

I wasn't doing ecstasy
The drugs weren't making me happy
And the beast, the *rage* in me
At life for taking Mike
At myself for taking drugs
Roooaaaaared!!!

I shamed and judged myself
In the days that followed
After each episode

I couldn't escape
The mentally and emotionally abusive
Relationship I was now in
With myself

Addicted to escaping the reality
It didn't matter what substance did it
The mental and emotional pain
Was all too visceral
The drugs, a moment of morphine
From the cancer metastasizing
My mind and heart

And after each binge
The reality became darker
Quite literally too
When my light bulb went out
Sometime after the first binge
I didn't even have the desire
Or energy to change it
I didn't care
It was too bright anyway
To be honest
I didn't even know how to change it
It was one of those specialty bulbs
That needed tools to even get in
Dante always did that sort of thing
If felt too complicated
My brain could not function
Short-term memory loss
Prevented me from doing much
I would try to do something
And boom
Completely forget what it was
No trail even to trace and remember
Gone
I would get so angry with myself

'*Fuck*, what have you done?
So fucking *stupid!*
What are you doing?!'

Then walk the length of the apartment
In some primal attempt to get away
From the thoughts in my head
I was abusing myself with
It was all I could do in those moments
To try to keep the fears at bay
That bubbled up
That I'd done
Some permanent damage to my brain
So beyond a few ambient lamps
I began living in the dark
I began singing an altered version
Of "This Is Me"

I was not a stranger to the dark
I didn't want my broken parts
Hide away
I said
Be ashamed
Of allllll my scars
Run away—
Break me down to dust
I didn't think there was a place for me
My sharpest words cut me down
I had no strength
To send a flood
And drown them out
Except for a smoke screen
Of drugs from time to time

*

And that is what we call
The downward spiral

My mind went on autopilot
Continuing to make plans
To *escape*
To get out of the city
As soon as I could
Living in some illusionary future

My spirit slipped back down
To the River Styx
And tried to re-negotiate with death
To stay with Mike
And *be* the past

And the present reality
Well
That wasn't all that pretty
For anyone in NYC at that time
Especially anyone battling
The war with grief on a personal level
The war in the head on the micro level
Was being mirrored on the macro
The polarizing politics
Came to a boiling point after four years
And filled the collective consciousness
Of the country with pain
Outwardly manifesting as such *hatred*
Abusing It's soul

*

The fight for equality
From the senseless murders
Of Breonna Taylor, George Floyd
And countless others
Erupted in the streets
More people being hurt or killed
Neighborhoods destroyed
And turned into warzones

Broken glass
Boarded up windows
People literally dying all around you
Either from the equality war
Or the invisible virus war

*

Everyday
On a small densely populated island
Semi-trucks were being filled
With the human bodies
Of fellow New Yorkers
Mothers, fathers, sons, daughters,
Grandparents, friends, and neighbors
Doctors, nurses, essential workers
It was *chilling* to pass them
Wondering if they were *filled*
With corpses
Causing further trauma and pain
To the consciousness of the city
Just being *aware*
Of what was going on
Outside your door
Was enough

There were no trashcans on the streets
The helicopters
Were constantly swarming with noise
Fireworks went off
All through the night
Why?
I still don't understand
Humans being hurt or dying
From those too
All the noise *actually* mimicking
A war zone
And to those on the micro level

In their own internal battle with grief
From a loved one's Covid death
Their own near death
Or some other cause of death
Well
PTSD doesn't distinguish
And you are in a war zone
An internal and invisible one
With the stranger passing on the street
The threat becomes
A mental and emotional trauma

Every time I walked out my door
Stray "bullets" known as droplets
Could strike at any moment
And make me sick
Or dead
It was an *incredibly*
Dumbfounding experience
To live through in the city
That is an understatement
There are no words

*

And each time I did drugs
Was like another round of bullets
Hitting my skin
I fired away
Because that day
And everyday
I let the shame sink in
I wasn't bursting through the barricades
I wasn't reaching for the sun
I wasn't a warrior
And didn't feel at all
It was what I was becoming

*

The drugs
The shame
Were like turbulence
To the fuselage of my body
Making it weaker
And by the fourth episode
The plane
Simply plummeted to the ground
Lights out
I was helped to the bathroom
And as I was dragged along the hallway
I momentarily became conscious
But was out again
Before reaching the bathroom
I was helped up to my feet
To vomit in the toilet
Once I was let go of
I fell to my right like a tree
I was helped up again
Only to fall to my left
When my support let go of me
The functions of my body
Were shutting down
Like a computer in suspend mode
It was as though I was paralyzed
From the waist down
I didn't want to throw up
I insisted on being horizontal
But have no memory
Of the journey to the bed

Where "I" went after that
And how long it was before I returned
I don't know
Doctor's could tell me one thing
From a biological perspective

Drug specialists could tell me another
From that perspective
I will tell you plain and simple
What *I* felt
Separation
It wasn't so much as I saw a light
But rather, I was the light
Funneling into, piercing, and reentering
The side of a dense, dark, opaque mass
That was my lifeless body
Perhaps the physical form
Had a few remaining twitches—
Circulations of circuitry going on—
Like pedaling an exercise bike really hard
Before taking feet—the force—off
As the pedals keep spinning

I'm not going to defend
What I experienced
Of this stigmatized subject
And the way it happened
I'm also not going to allow
Anyone to tell me
Something about an experience
They, nor anyone else
Was a witness to
I know what life was like before
And what it has been after
That I'm happy to speak to

*

As "my" life force penetrated my body
It went to the center of my heart
Then out from there in all directions
Simultaneously
Filling up every inch
Of this costume known as Anthony

79

To the three dimensional stage
Of this play we're all in
On Earth

Once the life force reached beneath
The surface of my skin
I felt an *immense* chill
My eyes opened immediately
I was in a room I had not been in
Which added to the confusion
Of where "I" was
Who I was

I noticed a phone on the nightstand
The only familiar thing to me
Ok, I know *who* "I" am
That is "my" phone
'I *must* be having a nightmare
How do I wake myself up?'
The unknowing
Of what would happen next
Terrified me
I sprang out of bed so fast
Hoping that I could wake myself up

The walls and room
Rapidly swirled and shifted
It didn't seem "real"
Certainly, I was *not*
In the three dimensional reality
I'd known for forty-four years

'My god!' I thought .
'Am I dead?'

Shock and panic filled me
As I franticly tried to figure it out
'Was this hell?'

*

I stumbled to the doorway
Braced myself in its frame
And looked out into a quiet apartment
No clue where I was
I heard faint music in the distance
Running water

'*Who's* apartment is this?
Why am I naked?'

Then *horror* like I've never known
Struck like a train
I pressed harder in the doorframe
To keep myself standing

'Was there a break-in?
Had I been raped?
Knocked out?
Are *they* still in here?
Was *whomever* this apartment was...
Murdered?
Lying in a pool of blood
Somewhere else in the apartment?'

The fear that image produced
Caused me to pause
I was frozen and *horrified*
To take another step
And find out

'Keep moving forward,
Keep moving forward'
A voice repeated.

I stumbled down the hall
When I got to the bathroom

There he was
The man I had been with
Shaving
Nonchalantly
Like Pam discovering
Bobby in the shower
I was both Pam and Bobby
Learning *perhaps* I was not dead
But *still* I was not certain
Maybe we both were
The apartment felt
Like some strange realm or dimension
Amnesia persisted
That there was something called a building
Outside of these walls
Something called a city outside of that
Or all the other Russian dolls
Of state, country, continent, and planet
Outside of those

I continued down the hallway
To the bedroom
And sat on the bed
Turned my phone on
And pressed the home button
When it came on in the dark room
The bright light
And Mike's picture on my home screen
Burst at me with a blast of energy

'Oh my God!' I finally realized.
'I'm not dead, you are!
And I almost joined you!
What have I done?
What have I done?!'

*

After thinking of Mike
My next thought was my mother
A flashback went off like a bomb
Blasting me twenty-years prior

I was lying in my bed in my flat in London
After a night clubbing
When I was coming down from 'e'
I was thinking of my parents
Tying to empathize with them
As much as I could
What it must be like to lose a child
I could do it only to a certain point
And that was horrendous
I made a promise to them that night
Being accepted by them or not
If I came out
That I would do *everything* in my power
To choose life no matter what
And do *everything* I could to stay alive
To outlive them
So they would never
Have to experience pain like that again
Thinking maybe, *just* maybe
A gay son would be preferred
Over another dead one
The promise was kept to my father
But the shame
That I nearly broke it with my mother
Dumped on me
Like a truckload of cement in that moment
I looked back at Mike's picture
Then flashbacked to Amsterdam
When I met up with Mike after London
Then the darkness
Where I met you
Before the flashback ended
And I was back in Manhattan

81

Twenty years later

*

Had thoughts of suicide popped back in?
Sure from time to time
Wondered how I would do it
I thought about researching
If I could euthanasia myself
They allowed it for physical diseases
In some countries
It seemed perfectly logical
And only fair
To allow it for what I perceived
As cancer of the mind and heart
That I battled for five years
I simply wanted to understand
What my options were
We all have free will
My heart couldn't take anymore
Life froze it with Joe
Shattered it with Mohammad
And with Mike
Well, it felt as if my heart
Was being eaten out of my chest
Violent bite by violent bite
It's main artery nearly severed
It felt more humane to put me down

But the promise to my mother
Always got in the way
It *irritated* me that it did
Made me feel trapped
In some purgatory
Where I had to wish
Death would come to me
Happen naturally
Or accidently

Be careful what you wish for

*

'Snap out of it!
Being a dead rock
Is a pretty good rock bottom
Stop!
Stop this now!'
My broken heart pleaded with me
While it tried to bring my head
Back from living in the future
My spirit, back from the River Styx
Both to the *present*
All three out of alignment
Living a triple consciousness
In one body

*

Ohhhh
The days that it took to recover
After each episode of drugs
I wasn't twenty-four anymore
Dancing in a London club
Some days
If I got out of bed
And put food in my body
That was a successful day
Showering and/or brushing teeth
Super successful
Dishes remained unwashed
And filled the sink
Making a phone call terrified me
To interact with someone
Paranoid that they might "know"
Because I wasn't acting
Or speaking "normal"

Timid with fear
Sending an email
Paying a bill
These felt like monumental tasks
And if one got done...
Big accomplishment

On the other hand,
"Maintaining" life
And an all-is-well persona
With a friend
Or my mother on the phone
Was a needed escape
Fooling myself everything was okay
For some moments of time anyway
And incredibly draining
Because I wasn't being authentic
Especially when asked the dreaded question
"How are you?"
As the saying goes
You don't fake depression
You fake being okay

*

I tried to keep
Some physical contact with friends
The part of me that was trying to fight
Understood it was one step
To help depression
Although I was worried
They would see I wasn't well
But if I tried to smile, tried to laugh
My physical appearance
Might be over-looked
Maybe, just maybe
They wouldn't suspect

*

I thought of Whitney Houston one day
When I looked in the mirror
That performance
When she was *rail* thin—that was now me—
Everybody could tell
Something was not healthy with her
My big sister of art
Singing about love
Filling my young heart
With joy and hope for it

I remember thinking when she derailed
I did feel pity
But also slight judgment
How could she let herself go like that?
She had *everything!*

Well, life is difficult sometimes
That's how
Plain and simple
We do the best we can
We fall down
We get back up again
Sometimes
We fall again and again

*

I tried to escape into books at Lollino's
My neighborhood café around the corner
Once it was allowed to reopen
I began going twice a day
Once in the morning for coffee
And later in the afternoon
For their orgasmic gelato
Lollino even created

A S'more's—my favorite!—flavor
When I suggested it
He'd never heard of S'mores!
But created it for me
Made me feel special
It was a hot seller!

Did I need to go twice a day?
Did I need gelato everyday?
Maybe, it was a hot summer
On the surface
I consciously told myself
Small businesses suffered
And if I could pick one to help
In *whatever* small way I could
By going twice and being neighborly
Lollino's was number one on the list
I'd been going for three years
The owners and staff were great

But unconsciously I was attempting
To simply venture outside more
Push through any fears
Of being triggered
Lollino's was a safe bunker
From the battlefield
And so close
Small interactions—
"Hi, how are you? Coffee please."
Helped me feel
Part of the normal/new, surreal normal
World again
Then off to yet another world in my book

*

But nobody could possibly know
What was going on inside me

I was able to hide it well
For my own sake
And probably theirs too
Less so when a crying baby
A barking dog
Or sirens erupted

I remember Amp, one of the cafe owners
Apologizing once for a baby crying
That wasn't letting up
Thinking it was annoying me
As I kept looking back and around
It wasn't annoyance I felt
But anxiety
Though I didn't recognize that then
Rather an extreme restlessness
There was discord in the air
To my subconscious
Crying means distress
Something was 'wrong'
Fight or flight response kicked in
Not even understanding
That was what was happening

Everybody, the *entire world*
Is going through hell,' I thought.
I can't bother anybody with my problems
Nobody wants that added burden
Another sign of depression

*

I had stopped practicing yoga at home
People had come to *me* for their health
What kind of example was I now?
I knew a titanic amount of love
Would come from the Modo community
But it would be too much

84

And sink me
I wouldn't have known how to receive it
How could I admit what was going on
And still feel deserving of their love
So I withdrew
The part of me that wanted to give up
At times was winning
And didn't want theirs
Or anybody else's love
He was done with life

My scared inner child was so angry
So sad
Felt life had *really* crossed a line
Pushed him down too many times
He was taking his ball
And going to play with death
The oscillation between him
And the part of me that *was* trying
To be a part of humanity
Watched cable news
To remain an informed citizen of the world
To try and see the "other's" perspective
Big mistake...HUGE
It only added to the depression
Cuomo would get a chuckle out of me
Here and there
When he'd go off on rambling tangents
But laughter was rare...foreign...or fake

*

The part of me that made an effort
Participated in the 7:00 p.m. applause
For the essential workers
It was well deserved
And touching to be a part of
A bit of CPR to my soul

And easy to do from my window
Yet still stay hidden
In my dark lair with my darkness
Neighbors couldn't really see me
Except once
When Rainbow Fairy's mother
Came rushing into her garden to clap
I dashed behind the windowsill
But a bit too late, as I think she saw me
I was *so* ashamed
To be seen in my darkness
The scene of the crime
Where at times abuse was happening
Afraid people would just know
What was going on
I felt bad I couldn't even give
A neighborly moment of connection
As they had moved in recently
Even little feelings of shame
From something like that
Was compounded

Even more so
As the doctors and nurses pleaded
Through tears on my screen
Over and over again
To *stay* home
Make their jobs easier
I did try to listen
Respect what they were going through
And I did
For the majority of the time stay isolated
But when I went off to do drugs
I felt I failed them
And piled more shame upon myself

*

I did a lot of sitting
Or lying in bed throughout the day
Staring into space
Closing my eyes
Reminding myself to *breathe*

And that was where
Unintentionally
Whether I wanted it to or not
Healing *began*
With that simple act
Ground zero...breathe
And then
In the darkness
Behind my closed eyes
Listening
To only the sound of my breath
There was peace in the dark

*

And then you came
To my mind and heart
Because the majority of our time
Was in the dark
I don't know exactly when
Trauma messes
With the timeline of events
Maybe after my resurrection
When in those first minutes
The flashback brought me back
To Mike and I in Amsterdam
And then the dark
Where you made your appearance

As if your soul *knew*
On some cosmic level
That I needed your help

However far away you were
In my 3D reality
My heart called an S.O.S
Save-Our-Soul
I time traveled back for the peace
I felt with you in the dark
To not be alone in it
Anymore

The intimacy I was searching for
Out in the city
I found within
With you
Mirroring
Intimacy with myself
And I embraced it
Instinctively
Naturally
Because it felt so good
To have you in the dark with me again
To see me through
And remind me
Darkness
Can be peaceful too

*

And then
There was a *whole* month
Between rising from the dead
And the last visit with Voldemort
Yes
There was another

I went to visit my mother
Before going to Chicago
Where Mike lived
And our third amigo Ben

Whom I had not seen in years
I needed to go
Wanted to
And didn't want to

When I flew over Chicago
On my way to Michigan
I saw the city skyline
And it hit like a semi
Mike was no longer down there
Tears began to flow
And sadness was triggered...almost daily
As I looked through old pictures from college
Packed away in boxes at my mother's

*

It was strange to me
Why suburbia Michigan
Was acting so "normal"
Going out to dinner
Made me slightly anxious
'Don't they know there's a pandemic
Going on outside?
Why are so many people unmasked?
And *why* is it so quiet?
Where are the helicopters
The protesters yelling
The fireworks?'
Obviously, their experience
Was not that of New Yorkers
More separated by lawns
And less populated

*

I delayed my visit to Chicago
I lived there briefly after university

It was where I first had sex with a man
And it wasn't long after Joe died
It had been many years
Since I'd been there
It wasn't a particularly happy period
In my life
And the happy times I had there
Were with Mike
I was getting triggered
At the thought of being there

But I went for twenty-four hours
That was all I could handle
I saw Ben
We had our own private celebration
And remembrance of Mike

*

The next day I had lunch
With my cousin Kelsea
Who drove me around
My old neighborhood and Boystown
Just a drive by
That was all I needed
To make some sort of peace
With my time there
And with Mike
No longer being there
Then I felt agitated
My gut shouted '*go!*'
'Get out!'
Back home
Within my own four walls
Even before the plane landed
I could feel
An uncontrollable restlessness inside
I couldn't sit still in my seat

*

With their partner, when they're an adult

The part of myself that Mike gave to me
That I wasn't giving myself
That I hadn't figured out yet
Or realized
That there was even *something*
To figure out
Was unconditional love

But for most gay boys
It doesn't get delivered
There is an unconscious
Or conscious feeling from their father
That their son is different
And within the child, that they are different
A disconnect of how to connect
To validate

I had no idea
I relied on Mike for that
All those years
Up until the last couple years of his life
When I ended up doubting it
Even from him
Because I couldn't give it to myself
Gave up on myself
And assumed he would too

An empty hole that doesn't get filled
With unconditional love
Then gets covered with shame
As the boy grows, feels, and learns
He is "different" from other boys

It is by no means the father's fault
And doesn't imply there isn't love
Regarding the father's consciousness—
About what love is and how to give it—
Especially with generations like mine
And the ones before
With the influence of the culture
And religions of the times
That has imposed conditioned beliefs
About what a boy is
Should do
And be like

That small validation of
I see you for who you are
I accept you
I love you
Which is crucial
In the emotional development
Of all children
At a very early age
For boys
That piece that should come
From their father
To set the example
Of their first loving relationship with a man
Which sets the stage for all the others

And when the young boy
Doesn't meet that belief
Loved for whom they *are*
Expressing themselves as
At those very crucial early stages
Well, that's where it starts
This piece that isn't validated
Isn't loved unconditionally
A disconnection from themselves

Especially for young gay boys
It's even more important
In order to have a loving relationship

And knowing who they are
What *all* children should know
And feel they are
Love

*

I certainly hold no blame toward *my* father
I do know
From a letter written by him in 1992—
When I was sixteen —
Which I received after his death
That his "biggest regret"
Was that we didn't have more in common
But he would "continue to try"

He wrote the truth
We didn't have a lot in common
I don't have many memories
Of just him and I
Spending time together
But he did try
Simply by the fact that he wrote
My brothers and I letters
Throughout our lives
To leave us after his death
I mean
How *amazing* is that!
I learned at that moment
Something we *did* share
Was a connection as writers
And my father did provide
As he was conditioned to do
In his "role"
And way of showing love for family
The "male's" role taught
By the generation he grew up in
But the disconnect with my father

Had been created long before
At the *crucial*
Emotional developmental stages
—As with many gay men—
And was covered with shame

I told you how
Mike knocked on the closet door
And pulled me out
It was done with such paternal care
And that hole
I didn't even know existed
As I chipped away the shame to come out
Was validated by him
I see you
I love you

*

Perhaps that is why Freud said:
"A father's death
Is the most important event
The most heartbreaking and poignant loss
In a man's life."

When it happens
All men—
Straight or gay—
Have to give it to themselves—
Unconditional love—
Moving forward
Yes, my father's death
Was an important event
But there was acceptance
Through talks before he died
That this is what happens
It's the cycle that is life
If it works "properly" in human eyes

A parent before a child
Yes, there was a lot of grief
Around not having him here
To rely on for advice or help
This human being that provided
That I shared a home with
And was simply, *physically* near
For half my life
Now physically abscent
Of course it was a big deal

But for me
What Freud spoke to
I felt more with Mike
And the loss was compounded
By the fact that Mike was my age—
Putting my mortality in my face like Joe—
And that he slipped away unexpectedly

It created more painful layers
To keep pulling back
To get to the empty hole
I didn't know was there
Which needed to be filled
With love from myself
So, instead, the emptiness
Was escaped via drugs
Until I figured it out

*

Adding to the pain of his death
Was the loss of *the* confidant in my life
We both knew the other "fucked up"
From time to time
And because of that
We would have that needed, quick check-in
Straight to each other's core

"You doing drugs?"

"Nope, I'm good"

"You?"

"No, I'm good too."

"Good."

And even if I wasn't, or he
We could tell each other
Unconditionally
And for many years, we were good

When I wasn't *"good"* anymore
Because Mike wasn't around
I abused myself
For my reaction to his tragedy

That small piece, that check-in
Of unconditional love
Could no longer be given by him
I hadn't learned how to give it to myself
Or that I needed to
And without it
That little hole
That was never validated by myself
Grew to every inch of my body
The shame, disgust, and self-hatered
Spread like cancer
And was only relieved
For some moments of time
With my morphine, my chemotherapy
However you want to look at it
That I *needed*

*

After my time in Chicago
While on the plane
I *tried* to resist
I *tried* to fight the feeling
I oscillated about meeting the man
I had my near-death experience with
In Hell's Kitchen
Huh, go figure

I sent a text to him before the plane left
My heart *desperately*
Tried to convince myself

'Just go home!
Go to bed!
It will be late!'

The plane landed at LaGuardia
I turned on my phone
There was no reply from the man
There were hardly any people at the airport
Late at night and during a pandemic
It didn't seem the bus
Was running normally
I waited and waited
I felt so exposed
I wanted to hide

Underneath my breath
I had been swearing and pleading
Since before the plane even landed
Distraught rage rose from the triggers

'Fuck! Fuck! Fuck!
Goddamn it!
Get me home!
Pleaassse, get me home.'

I beat myself up
For acting like an asshole
No compassion whatsoever
I saw myself as a grumpy, miserable man
Impatient
Tired from traveling
So I thought that was all it was
Still not yet fully understanding PTSD
The anger
At *whatever*
Life, Michael, myself, drugs
All of it
Pain trying desperately to be released
Confused unconsciously
If it *was* released
What was left?
Of me?
Of my life?
And did I like what was left?
I identified so completely with it
As it was all I knew
So intensely
For those few months
So stuffed down repeatedly
And escaped temporarily with drugs
Anything but to be fully *felt*
And released once and for all

*

I eventually called an Uber
Again a wait
I was so frazzled & exhausted at that point
I put in the wrong address
Instead of Jackson Heights station
I ended up...well, I don't know where I was
That was the problem
I asked the driver about the station

91

He said across the street, then left
It wasn't
Or not the one I wanted
And when I got out
I realized it was completely wrong
I had *no clue* where I was

I became frantic
My phone was dying
I couldn't *think*
All the more so
From the loud music and voices
From people out
On the hot summer night
Partying and drinking
Which had me distressed to tears
Boom
PTSD full force
Being lost in Queens—
Only the 3D manifestation
Of how lost I felt inside

I was able to get another Uber
To Jackson Heights
Before my phone died
The subway was *sooo* very slow
And kept stalling
I rocked back and forth
Swearing queitly below my breath
Trying to keep it down
And the tears away
So afraid to be seen
'Losing it'

"Please! Please!
Come on!
Fuck! Fuck!
Go, GO!"

Finally after *three* hours—
What usually can be forty-five minutes—
I entered my home

'Go to bed!
Go straight to bed!
My heart screamed
It's 3:00 a.m.!'

But then
His text came
He was up
And the invitation
To join him was extended
The anger and pain
Escaped once again

*

Throughout the next day
I kept telling him
To kick me out whenever
I hoped he wouldn't
I wanted to stay
And just be near a body
Any...*breathing*...human *body*
He was gracious
Said he didn't mind if I hung out
As he went about his day around the house
And running errands

It was evening
After returning from the laundromat
When he entered
I was in the other room
I turned the corner to find him
Sitting on a chair near the door
Staring blankly ahead

It was a look I recognized in myself
All too well
From Joe
From Mohammed
From Mike
Now reflected back to me
From someone else—a stranger really
Bonded by this feeling
Shock

"What happened?" I asked.

"I just received a text
My ex is dead
From an overdose."

I rushed to sit next to him
Put my arms around him
And *squeezed*
Kissing him
All over the side of his face

Something unconscious in me
Slowly began rising to my awareness
He was me
Three months ago
I was not in his current state
Perhaps not in the best of states myself
But there was progression
From where he was at
With such fresh news

I stayed until a friend arrived
Then excused myself
To go home and ground
I promised to come back
And hold him through the night
If he desired

He did
So much was coming up
From my own experience
To his
The war with mental illness
Claiming people left and right
Including nearly myself a month prior

*

That was when I *began*
Turning a corner
I entered my home
Both shocked and exhausted
By what had occurred

'I have to clean myself up,'
I thought.
'I *have* to be in a good head space
To be available for this...stranger
I could help him.'

I had experience—unfortunately—
I could be of service
It felt like a *tiny*
Bit of purpose for my life

'Oh yeah, it will probably be good
For me to clean up too,'
I laughed to myself
Before becoming *irritated* with myself
Questioning *why?*
Why was I *so quick* to give...a stranger
Compassion for his tragedy
While I was beating myself up
For a *reaction* to my own?
That was fucked up thinking on my part
I had to turn the corner

93

From self-judgment
To compassion
Immediately

I returned to hold him that night
As promised
Needing it just as much as he
If not more

*

That first month was challenging
I *really* wanted to be there—
If he needed to talk
Through any feelings or sadness
But it was a tricky balancing act
We'd make plans to meet
And I'd cancel
As my experience of grief
My own healing still unfolding
Would get triggered

But I stayed connected
Through texts of support
Checking in
Anything I could say
Just to let him know
I was there to listen
If desired

I knew if I went to him
I would probably end up doing drugs
Even though I did feel
Enough
Strongly
I still wanted to protect and respect
My own healing from the potential

I began waking up before the sun
And going down with it
Wondering if
A circadian rhythm reset
Would help
I was desperate to try anything
I felt rocky much of the month
As I concentrated on peace

*

Rays of strength would surface
Here and there
Bonding to others' trauma and sadness
The first in watching
Senator John Lewis' funeral
They played a portion
Of a song he sang in church

"I'm so glaaaaad
Trouble
Don't last
Always
Oh Lord,
Ohhhh Lord."

I would sing it over and over again
Underneath my breath
Walking around the city
The song acted like armor
From the landmine of triggers
Out in the city
And on days
When I was feeling...pretty good
The whispered singing grew louder

*

The next lighthouse flash came
After the explosion in Beirut
An elderly lady was interviewed
She had lived through
The Civil Wars of the 70's and 80's

"Each time these tragedies happen
We stand up and start again," she said.

Her words, a clarity through the darkness
She, to me, an instant hero

'If she can do it
I can,' I thought.

I jumped out of bed so fast
To write her words down
Before I forgot them
And taped them on my wall
They were followed days later
By a Lebanese man's words
Spoken with *such* strength
And unfaltering belief

"We will rise, we will *always* rise!"

*

Audra Day singing "Rise Up"
Was played over and over
In my apartment
Along with Peter Gabriel's
"Don't Give Up"
A song I turned to
Back in the pink birdhouse
In the months spent preparing to come out
Mary Calvi, a local news anchor
Was another unsung hero of my healing

In the beginning of the pandemic
She did a quick PSA
That played over and over and over again

"You are not alone," she would say.

Before she shared information
On how to reach out
For help with mental illness
Caused by the pandemic

When I first began hearing her
It triggered the bitterness
I was feeling toward life
Not long after Mike and doing drugs
I would try to change the channel
Before Mary could say it
But sometimes I wasn't quick enough
I heard those four words
Over and over again

'Yes Mary,' I sourly thought.
'I am alone.'

But as I became more gentle with myself
My perspective changed
I began finding comfort
In Mary's words
Once I *felt* her compassionate tone
With which she expressed them
As they penetrated my subconscious
And began subliminally soothing my soul
More and more
Like a loving big sister popping in
Reminding me
Making me feel
I was not alone

All of them poked
More holes in the darkness
Although sometimes
They'd get covered up again
When triggered out in the city
Making *any* progress
Feel erased

*

I stayed isolated inside during the day
Afraid at the height of city activity
There would be more chances
Of getting triggered
As had happened
On more than one occasion

Like a busy Union Square
Farmer's Market day
Where the only part
Of a passing conversation I heard
Was, "My best friend died."
And *boom*
Tears flowed that wouldn't stop
No sunglasses to hide behind
Exposed
And a mile away from home
So hidden most of the day
I remained

*

The dark nights and mornings
Were more peaceful
Going into the dark behind my closed eyes
And turning to you
Was more peaceful
Peace

In my inner and outer world
Was the priority
As well as maintaining the façade
To the outside world
Afraid at any moment
I would crumble

I rarely left without smoking a spliff—
Ok, probably never—
To ease anxieties to walk out the door
In between chain smoking cigarettes
With full awareness
How horrible the virus
Was to the lungs
But worrying about the amount I smoked
Creating a potentially more deadly scenario
—If I got the virus—
Was much lower on my list of priorities
Faaaarr behind
Just getting through the day

*

Three weeks prior to passing you
I finally had the breakdown
That needed to happen
Had been *wanting* to happen
Before drugs interceded
And prevented it
Having been afraid to feel the pain
In its entirety
Not understanding that being triggered
Was a *good* thing
Something needed to come up and out
In order to be released

I woke before the sun
Hopped on a Citi Bike

And headed toward the Hudson
As I rode the trail along the river
I began to cry
Once the tears were flowing
I had to pull over
Because I couldn't see properly
I turned off the bike path
Toward the river
Just south of the Christopher St. Pier
And went to the water
I got off the bike
Grabbed the railing
And for a *split* second thought
How *easy* it would be to jump in
Let the current...just take me

Instead I *wailed* out to the water
My cries orchestrated
With the lapping waters
In the silence before sunrise

I began to get angry
For losing it
And wanted it to stop
I was so confused

Why?
Why was this so painful?
What was *wrong* with me?
I turned toward the city
Took some steps away from the river

"So, if you're mad
Get mad
Don't hold it all inside
Come on and talk to me
Now..."

"FUUUUCCCKKK!"
I screamed to the tiny island I felt trapped in
"FUUUUCCCKKK you life!!"
And to the heavens for sending me back
Into the body I also felt trapped in
"What the FUCK is happening?!
What the FUCK is the point?!!
Who the FUCK am I?!!!
FUCK!
FUCK!
FUUUUCCCKKK!"

I dropped to the ground
Curled into a ball
And covered my head with my arms
In some primal effort
To try and conceal
The rage coming out of me
Shame kicked in
I reverted back to crying
And into deep talk
Within myself
Where all the answers already lie
And all that I'd want to hear
From my best friend

'I'm never going to be
In a relationship in this state .
Nobody is going to love me like this.'

'That may be true
...Or
Until you do meet someone
Somebody should love you until then
It might as well be you
Don't ya think?
You are with you
24/7.'

97

'Ughhhhh,
But that means I have to spend
At least a year with myself
I don't know who the fuck I am
After Mike
After my near-death
After relationship
I don't want to spend
All that time with myself
I don't like myself very much
Or how I've treated myself.'

'So rise up
Forgive yourself
Get back on the bike
Keep moving forward
And make a new choice.'

*

That's what I did
For the twenty-one days
Before seeing you

Everything that I thought I was
Was stripped away that morning
And the fear of what remained
Fearing there was nothing left
Had me blinded
To what *actually* remained
What has always remained
And what coming into contact
With you that day
Reminded me unconsciously
And reflected back to me
Love
That's all
All that I am

*

Do you realize?
How *incredibly* magical it is to me
That *twice*
After my darkest days
The brightest star
You
Appear
Shining!
Reflecting love
It is a miracle to me

*

Do you want to know
What *was* going through my head?
Before we passed that day?

It took me awhile to leave the house
I was feeling anxious
It was later than I liked to leave
But I had been reading
An *extremely* helpful book
That shed valuable insight
Into the gay experience
Called *The Velvet Rage*

It gave a relatable understanding
Into how from an early age
Young gay boys get damaged
By that element
That doesn't get validated by fathers
If it's not understood and healed
Then it follows them into relationships
As it had me
I felt some level of healing
But, I was reading a copy

I gave to Dante years prior
Perhaps we *both*
Should have read it together

I like to highlight what resonates in a book
I didn't want to highlight his copy
For days
I avoided going to the village
To get my own
That day
I told myself
Was *the* day
My *only* mission
To go out into the battlefield

I smoked a spliff
Walked to the door to get my shoes
Then turned around and walked back
I procrastinated with chores—
Straightened up, did some dishes—
And began feeling more comfortable
To stay home
2:00 p.m. was "late" for me to leave

'Come on
Just go to Three Lives
Get the book
Come home
Easy-peasy
It's helping you *heal*
Think of it as your medicine right now
That you *need*
You're nearly *finished* with Dante's copy
You're just going to start reading it
All over again
You can do it!
Maybe Troy will be there
He's always *so* nice and kind

It will be an *easy* interaction
Then you can come home
And you don't have to leave
For the rest of the day.'

I walked back to the door to try again
I knew my inner guide
Was trying to help
But it felt like pressure
And made me more anxious
I turned around
Went back inside
And rolled another spliff
To help with the new anxiety
I smoked it
Put on my shoes
And left at 2:30
Once I stepped out of the building
And saw how beautiful of a day it was
I relaxed

'Ahhhh.'
I sighed relief.
'I *can* do this
Go to the store
Buy the book
Come home
Yes, I *can* do this.'

Then I put one step in front of the other
I noticed you walking toward me
Near Starbucks
'He's not from around here,'
I thought.
'He looks, *brand* new—'
Like a Ken doll fresh out of the box
'Yes, definitely a foreigner.'

You got
Closer

'Wow!' I thought
'He's *stunning!*'

I looked up at the sun
Unknowingly
To compare the two of you
Yes, you were...*shining*
Glowing, as they say
I was seeing your aura
I've never seen an aura before
Nor understood that *was*
What I was seeing at the time
The sun *was* bright
But not quite as bright as you
Light was...
Definitely
Coming *from* you

'Yes, he looks European.'

You drew
Closer

'Wow!
He's reaalllyy hot!!'

I felt my eyes bulge
And my eyebrows rise
Unconscious it was the type of eye bulge
That comes from the soul
Bursting
From recognizing a mate
Shooting out my soul's windows
And well...bulging

'Guys that I find *that* hot
Are *never* interested in me.'

Ba Boom
Boom
Shows you where my self-love was
Nowhere

'Actually...
He looks Dutch.'
We passed
'Actually...
He looks like...'

Well...
You know what happened next

*

Once I turned the corner
I stopped in front of The Joyce Theater
I was so frazzled from the flashbacks
That I tried to run from—
Not from you—
But from myself
Again
Like I had run twenty years ago
Not from you
But myself
And being gay
Once I was back to the present moment
I tried reorienting myself
About where I was
And what had just occurred

'No, no, no!'
I frantically thought
'It *can't* be him.'

You
'It *can't* be him
Not *now!*
Not like *this!*
He can't see me like this
No, no,
NO!'
I went into denial
Completely convinced myself
There was *no way* it could be you
And I did
Or my brain did
Later did I learn with trauma
The brain can convince itself
Into denial
With experiences it can't handle
Then I carried on to Three Lives
For my book medicine

*

How ironic
If it wasn't for the trauma
The procrastination
With leaving my apartment that day
At that *exact* moment
We wouldn't have crossed paths
And
If it wasn't for the trauma
I would have run to you
Wrapped my arms around you
And jumped for joy
Nonetheless
The triggering happened
For something to be brought to the surface
To be healed and released
In the months that followed

Which took a big leap forward
A couple weeks later
While visiting my two-year-old niece
I was coming out of the bedroom
On my last day there
After a beautifully bonding visit
With this precious little human
Who was still learning who I was

Elodie was standing outside the door
As soon as she saw me
With pacifier in her mouth
She was still able to beam
The *biggest* smile—the talent!
She came running toward me
Arms stretched out
And literally leaped like a frog
Into mine
I was blissfully shocked
My heart melted
'Wow!' I thought.
'Somebody loves *me* like *that?*
There must be some value in me.'
Hard for *me* to believe
That was where I was at
With thoughts on myself
But it was
That's how you express love
The wisdom of a 2-year-old

*

About a week later
I had an appointment
With an intuitive healer
A real...star
Who helps by moving energy
From emotional blockages within

That develop from avoidance
And assists with the awareness
Of what needs to be addressed
In order to harness your power
And shift your perspective
Although I was clueless
To all of that at the time

I went in to address...
Why?
Why couldn't I let go
Of *specifically*
You?
For twenty years!
Even when I *did*
You came back in dream
Why?

Why did my subconscious
Use *your* image
In both happy and sad times?
Or how you showed up in a 3D *sighting*—
Or a strong resemblance
Of you and your energy—
At times I had been wondering about you
To the most recent "sighting"
Why?
Why?
Why?

Why couldn't I approach?
The limiting beliefs
I held about myself
After each encounter
Created two equal poles of a magnet
Preventing contact

Yet you came back

For *years* as inspiration
So I surrendered to that aspect of you
And found *acceptance*
In you
As my muse
If I moved to Amsterdam or anywhere
And we bumped into each other...
Awesome!

*

But
Like a starfish's reach
Trauma had spread
To all parts of my body
Hardened and pressed *everywhere*
Beneath my skin
The pressure of that blocked energy
Built to the edge
Ready to *explode*
But like a boa constrictor in reverse
It tortured me to the point
Of wanting to go to sleep
Forever
Eject
Out of my body

Through
Possibly magic
The Star
Guided our discussion around Mike
And my near death
And gently collected it all
From beneath my skin
Compassionately compressed it into a ball
To be integrated
Transmuted back
Into *something*

When we arrived
At the darkest kernel
The guilt around myself and Mike
That I let it happen
Again!
I was so *angry* at myself
For not trusting in his friendship
To turn to him
All that time I let pass
To connect
Until I was better
I hated myself for *that*
It felt like I lost
The solider by my side
Of nearly twenty-five years
In the war against mental illness
And tears burst
Like a hole in a dam
A stream beginning to flow again
I just needed to go with it
Continue to poke holes in it
Feel, release
And continue to heal

The journey with The Star
Flowed back to you
It still *bugged* me
Why couldn't I let go?
Of wanting to meet you?
There are *billions*
Of people in the world
But...
"I want to meet him," I said.
"I can't let it go.
That's my dream."

*

After the session
I felt less constipated energetically
It was just the beginning of the process
As the healing effects
From the shift in energy
Continued

*

I moved forward
Deciding when and how
I would move from NYC
Amsterdam and the world wasn't appearing
To be opening anytime soon
I felt the need
To at least
Get out of New York
We had a good run
But it was time we broke up

*

I had a week on the Cape
A time-share
My friend Bryan wasn't using
Who kindly offered it to me
My health was improving
But was not 100%
I was fatigued
The time away helped me comprehend
What I had been through
And when I returned from the Cape
I decided to stay grounded
In the stability
B12 had provided
For eleven years
To *properly* heal
It was *no* time to uproot

I felt lighter with the decision

The same person

*

The next time I went to the cafe
I described you to Amp

Upon my return
I went to Lollino's
While reading my book
Amp approached me
He asked if I would mind
If he introduced me to someone
He said the man
Had just moved to the city
From
The Netherlands
And didn't know anybody
He thought the man and I
Might like to speak
Because of the Dutch connection
And the fact that we were moving
To the other's country
Well
My move was delayed
By a pandemic

"Yes of course," I said.
"I always enjoy
Meeting a Dutchman."
It wasn't until
A few days later
It dawned on me
I wondered
If the new Dutchman in the 'hood
Amp wanted to introduce me to
And the man I passed on the street
Weeks earlier—
That *looked* brand new—
Whom I *felt* was you
Was perhaps

Yes
It sounded like the same man
"What is his name?" I asked.
Wondering
If after *twenty* years
I was *finally*
About to learn it
But Amp said he didn't know
Just that he moved here
From the Netherlands
He's a doctor
Who was looking for a home
In the West Village
But found one
In the East Village

*

Lollino's was closing its doors
A few weeks later
Amp said the man
Typically came in mid-afternoons
So yes
Up until the last day of the café
I was there in the afternoons reading
But then began writing
I figured
If I didn't run into you
Before Lollino's closed
And I ended up traveling
Or moving to Amsterdam in the New Year
I would simply write you a letter
Give it to Amp
Ask him to give it to you

If you ever came in
When Lollino's re-opened in the spring
At a new location
It seemed like a long shot
But it was something to try
And all I could think of

When you go after your dreams
No matter what it is
An opportunity is an opportunity
Doesn't matter how long or short
A shot it is

And what began
As a simple letter
To say, "Hi.
Is it really you??"
Turned into a play

I was curiously inspired
Again by my muse
Well
What *would* I say to Him?
To you?
To *possibly* the new Nederlands Dokter
In my neighborhood
After *twenty years*

The words flew out of me
Everyday at Lollino's

'What are we doing?'
I asked myself.

'Writing for the stage.'

'We don't know anything
About writing for the stage.'

'But that is what we are doing.
That is the answer to your question.
Just write!'
And the vision—
To make a one-person-show
About that first conversation
With first love
After twenty years
Magical sightings
Beautiful dreams
And a sprookje
Of a man looking for his first love
—Began

Your presence, your energy
Inspired me so much
I was *writing* again
Exploring and learning
A whole new medium

*

When the inspiration struck
This place I had entered
The other side of the dark
Where my future self
Was waiting to celebrate
And merge
Such a brilliant, creative surge of light
Blasted!
Infused me to be alive
To have a second chance

*

One of the regretable layers
Of Mike's death
Was that *if*

We ever did meet again
I wouldn't be able
To introduce the two of you
Mike would be so proud
That *he* was the reason
I met you—my muse

But the pain and darkness
From Mike's death
That The Star
Helped to forage and squeeze—
The coal of shame
Had been compressed
Into a radiant diamond
Where only love remained
For integration and release
For the two shining stars
In my life through the dark
All the love for you both
Poured onto the page
United together
Forever in art
Where you do meet
Immortally

Seeing you again
Mirroring me
Helping me to see myself again
And remind me
Like twenty years before
That
I am love

Something beautiful
Came out of 2020
Afterall

*

From winter through spring
I dove *deep* inside
Made healing my full-time job
With my therapist
As my only
Consistent weekly contact
Beyond niceties in a café or market
To maintain life
Or an occasional visit with a friend

It was like going back to school
Writing the play
Reading up on everything
From compassion and self-hate
To trauma and PTSD

Bessel van der Kolk's
The Body Keeps the Score—
Became my bible
With his well-crafted explanation
About the brain and how
The physical, mental, and emotional aspects
Are so intrinsically connected
When one has been traumatized

Much credit goes to veterans of Vietnam
Through extensive studies examining
Their stories of losing
Their fellow soldiers in battle
That they couldn't let go of—
That replayed over and over
These stories bonded them together

It was a new discovery
Under the umbrella of mental illness
And these symptoms needed
A new diagnosable label
That differed from the original

Classification of schizophrenia
Henceforth, it was called
Post-traumatic Stress Disorder

*

My father suffered from PTSD
He fought in Vietnam
He lost friends in front of his eyes
He was one of the "luckier" ones
To be able to maintain a life
Raise and care for a family
In unity with my mother
But he suffered and hid it from his children
My mother the only witness
As she later shared

It was something else I discovered
My father and I had in common
Losing friends in a battle
Having PTSD

*

As I began down my own road of discovery
I learned through my experience
What a ticking time bomb
PTSD can be
I started with the simple question
Of 'Why?'
I *had* to know why
I couldn't turn around
And say 'Hi'
That time
To make such a long-standing dream
Come *true!*
To simply *meet* you
I *had* to know

What happened
In that moment?

As the flashbacks
From that moment resurfaced
I was able to create
Some sort of a timeline
From the puzzle pieces
Scattered over the months
That came forth since Mike's death
I became the forensics scientist
Of my own death—
Symbolically on Juneteenth—
When the chains were first struck
Attached long before Mike's death
Long before childhood
Before my own birth

The abusive
Limiting beliefs, fears, and doubts
Of who I was
What I could be
Who I could love
What love…even was
Shackled to every cell of my being
All of it ingrained
Through mental and emotional genes
Links in a chain passed down
For generations
From cultures, societies, religions, & family
It was a death to *all* of it
Crumbling like the Twin Towers
That dark, quiet morning
Along the Hudson

*

As I crawled out of the rubble

To "stand up and start again"—
I was *bewildered* by what was left
To rebuild a new foundation with
You
Came walking down the street
And reminded me
Of the peace and love
In the dark
To rebuild a foundation from that

Did you know?
After 9/11
The Netherlands gifted New York
1,000,000 flower bulbs
To cheer the city up

As I look back
From passing you to this moment
You were those one million flower bulbs
Fresh from Holland
Delivered to me
That 16th of September afternoon
Right to my street
Planted in my soul
After passing through your aura
Weeks after
My Twin Tower tumbled
And as summer changed into autumn
And autumn into winter
The bulbs began to bud

*

I began meditating morning, day, and night
Making it part of my work day
Gradually increasing the time
Up to two hours a day
Sometimes your image would pop in

You began coming back to me
More in dreams too

Again as always, lovely to see you
Finding acceptance and gratitude
In the unconventional
Energetically-charged
Connection
These inspirational dream "sightings"
Sublimated the desire
To meet you in 3D again
I thanked you for the encouragement
To keep healing
Like an old friend
From long ago
As music and YouTube videos
About love and positivity
Began filling my apartment
Whitney, George, Celine, Barbara
Martin Garrix, and more
All welcomed into my home
I was singing *and* dancing
In between writing
Having entered a blissful period
Within myself
After the darkest night of my soul

But *only* within my four walls
As soon as I stepped out the door
The tension rose
My guard went up
It confused me at first
Still not understanding PTSD fully
Why was I able to be one person
Singing and dancing
Feeling happier
Alone
And a completely different one

Out in the city

I had to relearn
How to simply *be*
In the world again
So I began to make attempts
Here and there

*

One community minded New Yorker
Named Tim Murphy
Began organizing a meet up
Every Saturday
In A.I.D.S Memorial Park
For people to simply
Gather and talk
For a couple hours
To come together
Out of isolation

For weeks I thought
It would be good
For me to go
Week after week after week
I didn't
Each time I saw the postings on Facebook
I told myself,
'Next week, I will go.'
And one Saturday, I did
To the outskirts of the park anyway
When I saw the group of people
Talking and smiling
I felt intimidated
And walked by
Then forced myself to turn around
And go back
But walked by again

I got *so* frustrated with myself
Feeling like such an outsider looking in

'You're here, just go, *of course* they will be
Welcoming and nice,'
I told myself.
So I turned around again
Only to do a third pass-by
Then gave up
It felt like too many new people at once

'So you're not ready
Accept where you're at
It's okay
Be proud you tried.'
I thought to myself
Before carrying on to the East Village
To date for a new café
With the hope to bump into you
After Lollino's had closed their doors

*

Small interactions with the barista
Before escaping
Into reading or writing
Provided a put-my-feet
In the pool of life again
But not my entire body
To interact too much
Beyond ordering coffee

While I embraced the healing and joy
Working on the play was providing
I began to realize
Huh, you did it again
Happiness was beginning to bubble up
New creative inspiration and stimulation

With a new neighborhood
I hadn't spent a lot of time in
And new people to meet
I was like a three-year-old
Going to a market for the first time
Thinking, 'Wow, what is *this?'*
A baby phoenix rising
After isolation
From a pandemic, from trauma
It provided tiny bits of excitement
To push through little fears
Like each casting I did in Cape Town

*

One day I went into a children's store
To buy a gift for sweet Elodie
Normally in a store it would be
'Hi, just looking, thank you.'
But *something* in me wanted to connect
Felt safe to in that moment
And the owner and I did…on kids
Easier to do
When sharing
One of my favorite subjects
Elodie

I wanted to keep the conversation going
Our rapport built
I felt lighter inside
And when I left the store
I paused on the street
A streak of excitement ran through me
'I did it!
I had a conversation with a stranger,'
I thought.
It made me happy, proud,
A mini-celebration

It also made me feel a bit insecure
If I shared it with anyone
Beyond my therapist
The crazy look and thought I might get
That I was projecting I would get
"Big deal, you talked to a stranger,
You're forty-four years old."
But to me
It really was a big deal
Phoenix
Two steps forward

I had to learn how to be kind to myself
Because I was fighting and healing
From a battle no one knew anything about
Which helped to remind me
To do the same for others
Especially with the awareness
Of a pandemic still going on
That had—and was continuing—
To traumatize millions

*

As I explored the new 'hood
Just the thought of running into you
In the East Village—
Or *somewhere* in the city—
Of one of my dreams
Potentially soooo close
To coming true
Rocketed me to the moon!
And out of the depths
Of wanting to give up on life
Only months earlier

Yes!
I'll stick around

A bit longer
For another dream to come true

It pushed me through fears to go outside
Made it easier
To interact with the world again
Knowing
You could be there

*

Yeah
I usually still smoked a spliff
To go outside
But I *wanted* to be outside
I wanted to be in the *world*
More and more
The oldest dream at my fingertips
Created more healing as a by-product
Extending my comfort zone
To join and interact
With *life* again

Love:
"The will to extend one's self
For the purpose of nurturing
One's own—
Or another's—
Spiritual growth."[1]

You extending yourself
All those years ago
In what may seem
Like such a small and brief way
Has been rippling...forever
It continued to nurture growth in
And inspire me
All these years

To push through fears
Each sighting
Dream
To go look for you
To write a story and share
Intimate details
To heal

*

In the New Year
When the first draft
Of the play was finished
And sitting next to me on my couch
It was a bit lonely
I would have preferred you sitting there
Had I just been able to turn around
One
Of those times

I thought to my near death experience
And any regrets if I had died
Not many
Two really
Hurting my mother *of course*
The other
That I didn't get a chance to tell you
How you changed the trajectory of my life
Gave me my career and dream as a writer
By being my muse
My co-creator

I told my therapist
The regret
Was like *The Princess and the Pea*
I tried to cover the pea up
With mattress after mattress for years
To start new lives

[1] Quote from M. Scott Peck

Relationships and experiences
In England, the Netherlands
Australia, South Africa

She said she disagreed
I got *very* excited that she disagreed
"Really!" I said.
Feeling she was about to drop
One of her golden nuggets of wisdom
To expand my consciousness

"I see it as a pearl," she said.
My oyster secreting the nacre
Of all the beautiful people, places
And experiences
Over the irritating
Grain of sand—regret

Bingo
Yes!
Now that me oyster is cracked wide open
Here is my sprookje pearl

*

It was an enchanting period
Seeing you in dream again
But I was careful who to mention this to
Because of reaction in the past

"Don't you think he knows?
On some level
That it was special to you too?"
Friends would suggest over the years
When you came back up in conversation
Because I had another dream
Or potential sighting

I could feel their encouragement
As a friend
To let go
For my sake

And it's not like I didn't
Love and let go
Over and over again
But whenever I did
You returned
At some point
In some way
Plus ask *any* other artist
To give up their muse —
Especially a good one!—
Perhaps they would feel
It's not rational
To give up inspiration
That comes *to* you

*

Never give up on your dreams
Is what I always heard
No matter how silly it may seem
Or how simple
As meeting someone
You have no idea how to find

*

Back in the East Village
I began noticing love
Everywhere
In the form of graffiti
The word and inspiring quotes about it
Were on sandwich boards outside stores
Lampposts, trash bins, walls, doors
The sidewalk, police barricades

Everywhere!
It made me happy
I snapped pictures
Of every one I saw
Love was *definitely* in the air
Whoever the graffiti angels were
Tagging the city with their messages
Were brilliant...
Geniuses, really
To me anyway
I began feeling hopeful
For myself
For the world

*

Way back nearly a year prior
When the pandemic was just beginning
I prayed, I *really* did—
Having an understanding
Of going *through* tragedy
And coming out the other side
The strength and growth it could create—
That the universal tragic experience
The pandemic was becoming
Affecting nearly everyone
In some way
Challenging *them*
To choose life
Could make the world more united
More compassionate
With a collective strength to begin again

That wish was *quickly*
Extinguished and relinquished
Once the politics and protests
Added such hatred

But now, on the other side of my darkness
More and more everyday
And perhaps the world's as well
Love and light
Would begin to flood through
For more people
Like it had for me
And build
Once acceptance and healing
Had begun for them too
Adding it all
To a macro wave of love
A wave more peaceful

*

Now
Starting in the East Village
That was appearing to be true
And spreading through the city
It was what I was seeing
Everywhere
Love and magic

One of the graffiti quotes
I loved so much
On a lamppost in my neighborhood
Beautifully connected the two
"The only magic I still believe in
Is love!"

Of course I connected it all to you
Feeling positive, *finally,* we would meet
As you appeared more in my night dreams
And meditations
Life was feeling so romantic again

Excitedly I shared it with my therapist

Who again dropped a golden nugget
Pointing out everything I was seeing
About life
The love, the romance, the excitement
Was all just a reflection of me
That ultimately
'Sprookje' was a story about self-love

Yes, yes, intellectually
I understood
What she was getting at
But I didn't feel it in my core
I said I agreed
Could see that too
But 'Sprookje' to me
Was still a story to find the boy—
Now a man—from long ago
Reunite artist and daemon
My 'Boys in the Band' phone call
In the form of a play
To celebrate what we—
Artist and muse —
Created
Together

*

As I continued working with my therapist
I felt I needed an alternative route
My healing took another leap forward
To another galaxy, dimension—
Quite literally
When I did drugs again
One of the *best* decisions
I could have made for my healing —
A ketamine session
Under the suggestion and watch
Of my therapist and pharmacologist

You even visited me there

I had no idea what to expect
And no clue
How tremendously helpful it would be
With the trauma and PTSD
I *do* believe
In the positive benefits of drugs
For healing
As studies are showing
With ketamine, ecstasy, mushrooms
To help with all forms of pain

*

By the rebirth of spring
As Mike's anniversary approached
I remembered Rainbow Fairy
How vitally important she was to me
I sent her a book as a thank you
And a note to her parents explaining why
Before heading out of town
When I returned
There was another rainbow in the window
With a big
"You're Welcome" above it
Of course I had to comment
Taping a message to my window
What another masterpiece it was
And boom
We created our own
New form
Of social media
Through window art

*

Once my head and heart

Were doing much better!
It was time to concentrate on body
Get back in the yoga studio
And one day after class
Lying peacefully on the floor
I fell into a deep meditation

The silhouetted image of a face
Began coming forward
I assumed
It was going to be you
Visiting again
But was surprised to see
Once I could make out the image
It was not you
But me
It *was* all a reflection of me
Now coming from
And feeling it in
My *core*

*

I *had* met someone new
And began dating him in the East Village
Spending time with *him*—
The newest and best version of him
After everything that happened
All the choices I had made
All the good and perceived bad
Had created this new butterfly
Whom I was accepting and loving
Unconditionally
As the chrysalis continued
Falling away

The romance with myself
Showing me

What I am capable
Of giving to someone else—
Of being gentle and loving—
As I had learned to be with myself
Like attracts like

All that *time*
I was absolutely *dreading*
Spending with *myself*
All those months ago
Along the Hudson
I would not trade for the world
Now adding and making
The most difficult year of my life
Also the most beautiful and precious

The *adamant* desire to meet you
—That I couldn't let go of—
That I proclaimed to The Star
Was the desire to meet myself—
By loving all parts—
"Go find yourself
So you can find me."
-Your Soulmate[2]

*

The demons
That you hear people battling
I have
That is for sure
For many years
Yes, they were very real
Until I realized
They're just parts of myself
That needed to be loved
Through compassion
And self-acceptance

[2] Quote from Instagram, annonymous

To be and embrace
My most authentic self

And that piece that needed to be validated
Gets validated
Not by my father
Nor Mike
Or anyone else
But by me
It doesn't get more authentic
For me anyway
In my humble opinion
Then sharing being dead on a bed
And what brought me there

*

Traveling the globe and writing books
Coming out, having relationships
Showing young gay boys
That *this* love
Exists
Yes, they are all
Wonderful accomplishments
But pulling myself out of last year
Is the one most *dear* to my heart
In the current moment

*

I thought way back to Laguna
To the spring of 2004
When I returned
From the initial search for you
And *first began* writing our story
Before stopping at the ending
Because I hadn't found you
The thought did cross my mind

Perhaps
It was a story
About the existential search for self
I just needed sixteen more years
My muse, the East Village
Some graffiti angels
My therapist, Rainbow Fairy, and more
To add that one little word...
love

*

From Amsterdam
In the darkroom of Cockring
With you
To twenty years later
In New Amsterdam
On the Upper West Side with my therapist
And all the fairy tale characters in between
Back to the light

I felt like Richard Gere in 'Pretty Woman'
The bathtub scene
When he laughs at the thought
It cost him $10,000 in therapy
To say one little sentence
Yup, that was me...except for one word
Not to mention the plane tickets, editors
Printing and such
For the search
I don't even want to add it up
Regardless
It was a bargain
Priceless, as love is...
And magical

*

Hello
My name is
Anthony van Leeuwen
My first love
Whose name I didn't know
And searched the world for
Is Anthony

Here I am
Found
It only took forty-five years
And look out
'Cause here I come
And I'm marchin' on
To the beat I drum
I'm not scared
To be seen
I make no apologies
This is me!

*

As kindred spirit
Ms. Gloria Vanderbilt said—
We had a moment
At the National Arts Club
During a Fashion Week event—
I've never seen such elegant chicness—
She nailed it
She *was* Fashion Week

Man could that lady
Shoot a departing second look
Over her shoulder
Straight from her eyes
To yours
With a sparkle
A look of love to last a lifetime

That made you feel
Like the center of her universe
She knew
Love
Is
Everywhere
In every moment

If that's all we are
And "we're all one"
Then the illusion of the "self"
Of separation is null
And all that really *does* remain—
Is
Love

—I digress—
But if you're going to go off on a tangent
Gloria Vanderbilt
Is the tangent to go off on—
Anyway, and I quote her:
"We are not put on this earth
To see through one another.
We are put on this earth
To see one another through."

*

Everyone mentioned
In all my writings
You, they, are mentioned for a reason:
For helping to see *me* through
On Earth
To *this* moment
And for nurturing my growth

Thank you New York!
For not allowing me

To break up with you
For our best year together
You have my heart
Thank you Amsterdam!
You have my soul

*

I was first inspired
To write a story at nineteen
From a creative writing class
Second semester
Sophomore year of college
I wanted to write
The story of two friends
Two men
The *best* of friends
No clue I was gay
Or that I wanted to write a story...
Live a story
About the romantic love
Of two best friends
Who were both men

I didn't get very far
I picked their names
Chance and Gabe
If I remember correctly
But the desire was there
Which was enough
Plus twenty-five years
To set the dream in motion
For *these* words

*

I wanted to write about you
Before I ever met you

Or myself

Mike and I had just met that semester
Our pledge term for Phi Kappa Psi
About to embark
On our adventure together
The first person I needed to meet
In order to meet you
And then myself

Now that I have...*unconditionally*
I call out to you
Mooie Man
From the dark
To the light
To my dreams
To a summer day at the beach
To a spring day at the park
To a cozy autumn evening at the carnival
These
Our dates to me
Seared in my mind
Magic personified
Thinking of you
And you appearing
All leading you to my home
On 19th St.
On that shining summer day
Never
Did I imagine
*The Promise s*ung to me

If I wait for you
Then you'll come for me

I was coming for you
Until a pandemic stopped me
Probably the only thing that ever could

But you beat me to it

*

Now that everyone knows
That I didn't stop you
On the street that day
And that there was not confirmation
Of the other three sightings
All of which were during times
That you'd want a best friend
To show up and be by your side:
The saddest
The happiest
And the crossroads
Perhaps
That is not how I'm viewed by you—
As a friend—
That I could understand
But now I hope you know
That is how you've felt to me
All of these years

*

If you read this
Might you come forward
To confirm or deny each sighting?
Perhaps it's in these pages
You're learning of all my adventures
Since we last met
And not on the coast of Africa
With hundreds of candles for a setting
Like my dream many years ago
But now...you know

And...
Somewhere!

You are there
You're not an angel
Not a hallucination
But an *actual* human being
I'm sure of it
And *you*
Are the Dutch Prince
Of *Sprookje*
Whether you wanted to be or not
The muse of my own personal fairy tale
And love affair with life
That has been with me
All along
In the most incredible
Unbelievable ways
Encouraging, supporting, and inspiring me
With *magic* and *miracles*
Flapping your beautiful butterfly wings
Through one *very important* question
And answer
Long ago
Once upon a cozy December
Which created this tsunami
Of love and gratitude
Coming back to you
On the other side of the world
Or potentially...
From my neighborhood?

And
To you

Ring
Ring

Helllllooo!
Beautiful man from the dark

119

Best muse ever!

Are you there?
Are You there?

Thank you!

I love you!

You may retire as my muse if you like
With *full* benefits
Eternal love and gratitude
As promised long ago
In the pink birdhouse

Unless!
There is *another* sighting
Somewhere in the world
And inspiration
Strikes!

You know what?
Celine and Barbara
They are some very wise ladies
Singing to me all those months
Telling me
To
"*Teeeellllll him*"
To
Teeeellllll you
That the sun and moon rise in your eyes
And to reach out to you...

Because...

Love really IS
The gift you give yourself

Ok so
According to the point system
One point for making the call
Slash
Writing the story
Five points
For saying I love you
I'm at six points...
So far ;)

By the way...
What *is* your name?

I wonder...
—Talk about reflection
— Is it Michael?

Epilogue

Lost & Found: His Name

"It seemed important at the time," said the woman on the television as I walked into Ray's living room in Laguna one Sunday summer morning in 2005. It was a couple months before I left for Africa.

"Who's that?" I asked.

"Oh darling! That's Gloria Vanderbilt; she's fabulous!"

"Vanderbilt, like Gilded Age Vanderbilt?" I said, recalling the name from history class.

"Yes, that's the one. She was *the* girl, in the Poor Little Rich Girl trial in the 30's, with Gloria Vanderbilt designer jeans in the 80's," Ray continued.

"Yes, that sounds vaguely familiar," I said.

I was sure I'd heard about the case, or perhaps seen a commercial for the jeans as a child once upon a time. Yet, I had certainly never connected them to a face or the one on the screen before me.

"She's an artist and a writer, too," Ray added. "She's talking about her latest book: *It Seemed Important at the Time*. It's about all of her lovers over the years."

Now my interest was piqued, because she was a fellow writer, and someone who referred to her "gentleman callers" as lovers. I sat down to catch the rest of the interview. Afterward I was sold. Gloria's book went on my mind's reading list for...one day. She sounded like an interesting lady.

***

I returned from Africa after the second sighting of Him—Amsterdam Angel—and the idea of writing the book to find Him, was birthed. At that point, now freshly thirty, I had an insecurity that festered about never having had a long-term relationship. Being in the closet—both to the world and to myself—unconsciously prevented me from taking *that* next natural step with a girl in school or a woman in adulthood, simply because it did not *feel* natural. When I did come out, dating experiences never evolved to that coveted dangling carrot label—*boy*friend.

Writing the book was my idea of a way to find Him, yes.

I also wanted to prove—probably more to myself than anyone—that, no, I didn't have a long-term relationship or anything conventional. Yet, that didn't make my experience with Him any less poignant or special; love could occur over a few nights, one night, or one moment.

After having it ingrained in me by society and religion that I was *not* allowed to have same-sex love, it made it that much more precious when I did. Feeling safe, peaceful, and at home in someone's arms—no matter how long in the third dimension—billions could agree it's incredibly precious. Even if I never felt it again, I wouldn't leave Earth without *that* universal human knowledge. While I continued the journey of finding and knowing that safe, peaceful, and at-home feeling within myself, I also held onto the memories with Him—tightly—for twenty years.

Would I have liked the one-person-with-longevity experience? Yes. But it wasn't happening, so I valued the times when I did share intimacy in varied forms. Still, I felt insecure, although I didn't recognize this as such, rather I attributed the feeling to something missing from my personal history. Nor did I have words for why I valued the men that crossed my path.

I tried to view other encounters with men I met traveling the world as meaning *something*, no matter the duration of the acquaintance; whether a moment or many they were part of that journey. We were drawn together to reflect *something* to each other, to learn and grow in some way. They were lovers with whom I based my experience—and their potential—on what I had learned from Him.

Tossing the term lovers around in my head, while contemplating what I was trying to express with the original book, Gloria and her interview popped into my head. I went to the library and checked her out. Once I finished her book, I felt understood. Gloria put my feelings into words. I was comforted. I felt validated that the story of Amsterdam Angel—the person, our experience, the sightings, the dreams, the search—was special, and worth writing. An angel in her own right, Gloria helped sprinkle that sentiment into my consciousness as I began writing *Amsterdam Angel.*

***

By the time I moved to Manhattan in the summer of 2008, I had given up on the idea of the book, while I tried to belong and create a life in the city. Eight months later, in February 2009, I was the plus-one of my friend Douglas who had an invite to an art exhibit at the National Arts Club in Gramercy Park. I was still very green to New York City and felt socially awkward at such events as Fashion Week; that evening was no different with the grandness and history of the Victorian Gothic Revival brownstone as the setting. Along with what appeared to be "important" people of the fashion world and New York City nightlife who were mingling with me—a Mid-western flight attendant and a failed-before-even-trying-now-that-he-was-in-NYC-and-the-publishing-world-it-provided-writer.

Although my fashion was not something I felt awkward about but quite confident in and it helped armor my jitters. I wore an outfit I picked up on Melrose Avenue at the infamous, The Cosmo Show. One I had used in a shoot with Biron that eventually went on the zed card that got me to Africa. A California look represented in a New York setting, but in style is in style, no matter where it's shown. Yet my social anxiety still had me glued to Douglas' side.

The wine was free. So I had a few glasses to loosen my nerves, planted with Douglas on the outskirts, in my comfort zone—nearly to the wall, as flowers. In the center of the room with a gaggle of gays surrounding her, was Gloria, tilting her head back, laughing, as the gays tried to entertain her. They were magnets to her ultra-magnetic charm. Douglas and I couldn't take our eyes off her. Not because she was Gloria Vanderbilt; to be honest, I did not recognize her at the moment. I'd seen her image once, in an interview 2.5 years prior.

Regardless, we couldn't look away from Gloria. Her charisma and energy were alluring to all eyes that fell upon her. The room was hers. Every one of the guys surrounding her was wrapped around her finger. Douglas and I couldn't get over how stunning the woman before us appeared. Elegant. Exquisite. So very chic in black slacks, black shoes with a bit of heel, black blouse, all covered by the most stunning black cape—a work of art in and of itself—beautifully embroidered in fine detail. Simply topped off with a necklace and earrings that sparkled as her hair swayed with each thrown-back laugh of her finely featured face.

Gloria was busy with everyone else, so the shy me attempted mingling in this new world, after grabbing another glass of wine. Douglas and I separated. I decided to take in the artwork. Art didn't talk back. I didn't have to come up with small talk with it.

As I wandered the room, my eyes crossed paths with Patrick McDonald, "The Dandy of New York." He gave a nod as if to welcome me to have a chat, so I attempted to expand my comfort zone. I had met Patrick once or twice briefly. But by no means did I think he knew or remembered me. From the few interactions I had enjoyed with Him, I discovered Patrick was one of the most gracious people I'd met in the city's nightlife. I admired his talent for mingling. He possessed a gift for small talk with anyone and was so polite. His interest in whomever he spoke to felt genuine, even with me.

Only moments after we began chatting, she swooped in with her cape flowing behind her and a smile. Remind you, I still had no idea it was Gloria Vanderbilt. Only that woman, with such magnetism and style to die for, whom I had been admiring from afar, was now right in front of me. Gloria smiled as if needing no introduction, which she didn't, but unfortunately for me she did. I was bursting to compliment her outfit. The cape—although being uneducated to women's fashion, I didn't even know the proper terminology and thought it was called a cloak—was even more striking and impeccable up close. I wanted to wear it!

"Ma'am, you're outfit, the cloak, the jewelry, everything...perfection!" I said, as I kissed my fingers and opened them to the air. Why I did that I don't know. I'm not sure I'd ever even done that before—probably the wine. I was a little tipsy at that point. Gloria giggled, smiled, and said thank you in an almost whispered voice. Before turning and making her exit.

Of course I watched her depart. Of course a woman like Gloria probably knew people do. And that is when she turned and gave me a second look. She smiled, and her eyes squinted as if to laser focus on the target—mine. When she gave me a nod, her eyes—I swear—sparkled with light that shot to mine, connecting our energy for a moment. Something burst inside me, and I was taken aback. I didn't know what had happened. But something happened.

The following morning when I woke up, I sat upright in bed, hit with the affects of a hang over. Then that woman from the night before and our moment popped into my head. I couldn't get her out of my mind.

Why did she look so familiar? I thought.

Then it dawned on me. The woman from the interview in Laguna!

Oh, my God! That was Gloria Vanderbilt!

I was so bummed because I wanted to share how much her book helped influence *Amsterdam Angel*. Giving me a nod—like she did the previous night—to go ahead with it. Ohhhh, I was so disappointed to miss the chance to chat about writing with Gloria.

Then I remembered the look she shot me, felt it; I can still feel it. It was exactly what she spoke to in her book, love being everywhere: in a moment locked in someone's eyes, with a flower, with a fragrance. I was happy and grateful because Gloria and I had our moment of love with a nod.

And wow! What a second look! She knew how to work it, the hair and the cape twirling with her swiftness, and in heels, classic, eternal...a sparkling diamond cameo in my life. Now, I could get a second look from Gloria Vanderbilt, but could I get one from Angel with any of those sightings...nope.

Did the brush with Gloria inspire me to continue the writing? No! I was still *firmly* committed to giving up.

***

You all know what happened next. I met Dante six months later. He started encouraging my writing. I got inspired to make the series. And boom—began writing again.

Gloria also began coming to me in dreams as I wrote. I wish I'd written them all down, had I known I would write this one day and use her as a muse as well. Ahhh, that's the curse of a writer...when intuition says to write something down and I don't, because I have no idea at the time, what I would use it for. I remember thinking that I should archive the Gloria dreams because I found it so quirky to see her in them.

"I had another dream of Gloria last night," I'd say to Dante when I woke up before relaying it to him.

They usually involved hanging out with her at home, like girlfriends; seeing her latest dress, chatting about boys. In another, we were at an event in the city, a talk of some sort. Dante was there too. He and I were romantically canoodling and laughing in our world ignoring the speaker. Gloria and Anderson Cooper were in the row right behind us. Gloria was girly-giggling with pleasure to see our gay moment of love, leaning to her son to point out how nice it was to see gay affection in public. She certainly wasn't disapproving of our manners for not paying attention to whatever the talk was about. How could she be, she wasn't paying attention either.

On occasion, Dante and I would attend tapings of shows that were filmed in the city. We visited Whoopi and the ladies at *The View*, Meredith at *Millionaire*, and months before *Amsterdam Angel* was released, we got tickets to Anderson Cooper's talk show inside the Time Warner Center.

Days before the taping, the producers sent an email to audience members. They asked for volunteers to write in about a personal possession with a brief story of how it correlated to a loved one. The actress Marilu Henner was scheduled to be a guest on the show promoting her new book, *Total Memory Makeover*. Marilu has a rare ability to remember nearly *every* day of her life in detail since about age ten, in addition to many memoires prior. Her book shares insight into how people can exercise their memory. The producers wanted to use a couple of audience members in the segment with their item as an example for Marilu to explain memory-building techniques.

I wrote in about the last Christmas present I received from my brother Joe three weeks before he died, a CD of piano music by George Winston. I was chosen. The next thing I knew I was in The Allen Room overlooking Central Park, standing next to Anderson, telling the story to Marilu, before she explained how music can be one avenue of the senses to recall memories. Of course, as talk shows do, the audience received a copy of the book. I read it and, it *was* a really fascinating read. Buy it!

In the months that followed leading up to 12-12-12, I finished writing *Amsterdam Angel.* I experimented with applying the techniques I learned from Marilu in different areas of the story, and it really did work! I started remembering more about Joe and childhood. Dots connected and memories resurfaced that I was able to use in the book. Tip of the iceberg introduction, but the *experience*, of learning, applying, and seeing results were felt.

The following spring after my book came out I saw on television that Marilu was back on Anderson's show as a co-host. I was excited about what I had learned from her book and how I was able to apply it. I got a ticket to another taping. I hoped I could express my gratitude to Marilu for helping me remember more about Joe, and to give her—and Anderson—a copy.

I contacted the producer I had corresponded with on the previous visit. She loved the synchronicity of it and responded with enthusiasm. She wanted to try and surprise Marilu and squeeze me in at the end. She said she couldn't promise anything, as television timing goes. But she said she'd get me backstage afterward when they did a meet and greet with some audience members, if not, which is how it played out.

Of course! Marilu and her incredible memory remembered me. She gave me a big hug and was genuinely happy for me, a real angel on earth bubbling over with high vibrations. Anderson was equally positive and empathetic after explaining the personal connection of being around the same age with the sudden death of a brother. They both received their copy—a *special* limited stamped edition of *Amsterdam Angel.*

***

For me, it was about connecting on a personal level as I passed the book out to different celebrities that I crossed paths with on land or in the air. But not all, only if there was a kindred experience. Something that they might enjoy and relate to personally, whatever aspect of the story it was.

Alicia Keys received her copy after I served her one day while working a flight back to New York. Our connection was to Egypt. I'd read she had a mind-blowing experience with the country—enough to name her son after it. I also had an enchanting time learning about the culture and people from a kind local (Chapter 6!). With that connection, I thought Ms. Keys might like to "go back to Egypt" by reading another's account of a soul-expanding experience of a country that was dear to her heart.

I gave Armistead Maupin *Amsterdam Angel* one summer, and the second book, *The Reverie Bubble,* the following summer when I bartended his readings at The Crown and Anchor in Provincetown. Always so kind to me, Rick Reynolds indulged my geeky excitement to meet another writer and let me slip away from the bar after the reading. Mr. Maupin was pure inspiration and adoration, pioneering a gay series that led the way for something I never imagined I would attempt myself one day.

Famke Janssen, last to scurry on board one day—felt like a girlfriend, like Gloria—I could have chatted with her all three thousand miles across the country. With her, well, of course, there was the Dutch connection.

"Alsjeblieft," I said to her when I handed her tea then left. She had a cute surprised look not expecting to hear Dutch and stopped in the galley on her way out of the lavatory. We had a nice chat and she helped me practice a little Dutch.

She insinuated talking more a bit later in the flight and I hoped we would. Stupidly, I ran an order the next time she was in the lavatory; she was back in her seat by the time I returned.

Please pee again, Famke! Please pee again! I prayed she would before we landed so we could talk some more. She has *great* energy, very uplifting, and positive. She didn't pee again, and I didn't want to bother her. It always feels like a fine line when serving celebrities, respecting their privacy and not gushing over their work that you love.

What was I doing...networking? I was always uncomfortable with that concept, even though I could care less if someone asked something of me. If I could help in some way, I would. But I hated requesting something of someone else.

What did I want to happen, a tweet about the book? Sure it would have been nice to have help getting the word out. Or rather, getting the book in front of His eyes, like the plan was long ago when I thought Oprah and her book club would take care of it in a snap. But I didn't care about sales or money, and certainly not about notoriety.

A shaman I saw during that time period suggested a handful of European publishers that he knew, that he felt could be a good fit for the genre of my book... to a very unenthusiastic me. Of course, being a shaman, he picked up on the energy simply because I didn't respond much or add to his advice.

"Don't you want to sell any books?" he asked.

"Yeah, I guess," I responded. "Well, no, I really just want to sell one copy. And I don't even want to sell it. I only want to give it to Him, and ask, 'Is this you?'"

Yes, I wanted help. But more like the little bird from the children's book, *Are You My Mother?* I was wandering around bumping into celebrities asking/not really asking, "Will you help me find this blond hair, blue-eyed Dutch man?"

I feared success in the entertainment industry and expressed that to the shaman. Writing is show business for shy people. I was not interested in fame, Which usually accompanied success in the industry. We've all seen what fame has done to many, many people. I was more than aware of my past with substance abuse after profound, life-altering experiences. Add memoir into that, revealing intimate details of the darkness in my life, my reactions to it, and the thoughts in my head to be shamed or shunned, and voila, a sitting duck for triggers...kaboom!

Why would I want to put myself in a potential situation like that? I didn't need any conscious experiences that could trigger going down that road again. Was it worth putting my sobriety at risk for a dream? These were questions I asked myself.

Apparently, the why, was Him...the dream. It drove me, motivated me. If He stopped coming with inspiration maybe I would have stopped. But He didn't. So I didn't. I genuinely hoped as well in doing so, it might help someone that reads it, who may need to hear about someone else going *through* something, and seeing beauty again. It felt like such a *Catch-22*, that I went back and forth on for years, and that I would continue to do for years, leading up to *this* piece.

At the same time the creative *surge* and *bliss* to create, that He helped to inspire, was a—healthier—addiction in itself; exciting and challenging to execute, as well as healing. Plus, I had this dream, to say 'hello,' to meet someone again, for the first time—really—that wouldn't let me let Him go. As much as I tried for *years*, because He kept coming to say 'hello' to *me* in dream. I couldn't walk the streets of Amsterdam like I had before "looking" forever; getting the story out was the only thing I could think of. Seems like a convoluted way to find Him—I realize—all because...I didn't ask His name.

Well, as you all know now, it didn't take fame to trigger using hard drugs again after nine years. All it took was a bunch of tragedy and loss and pain and, and, and a perfect storm of it, you know the story—flip back if you don't—and *voilà!* Here we are, revolving door still writing and still being inspired by Him. Ahhhh, who are you Beautiful Man from the Dark!

***

2016 started with the notion and goal that the third book would come out on my 12-12 date that year. It also started with my father's brain cancer diagnosis a few weeks later. He died on 12-11, one day before the book was to be released. I had already scratched the launch a few months prior. Earlier in the year, I thought how great it would be that my father would *know* I put out *three* books before he died, for that triple-crown pride from him before he left this realm. Somewhere in me the *surely-that-would-make-up-for-being-gay* thought still lingered in my subconscious. Yes, I really had such thoughts after coming out to my parents.

I'll make it up to them for being gay, for not giving them grandchildren.

After overcoming the collective's "rule" of whom I could love or screw, I fell into the trap of another "rule", which allowed society to dictate who could have kids. At that time, at least around me, there were the rare anomalies of a few gay parents, which I saw after I moved to California. They had this aura of breaking the unwritten law. Something I could never be so bold to do, yet respected.

Yes, I'll make it up for being the stain on the family. I'll travel the world! I'll write books!

What. The. Fuck?

Fuck you Catholic Church and society for making me feel like I wasn't enough. Like I had to make up for this tainted—gay—piece of me. Yes, I said it and mean it, fuck you Catholic Church and your *Flowers in the Attic* poisoning of my young heart and mind. You deserve a class action lawsuit for mental and emotional rape of millions.

Making up for the tainted piece is what *The Velvet Rage* spoke to regarding the stage of shame—stage two—that many don't overcome in order to evolve into stage three. By coming out, many leave stage one, only to feel the need to "make-up" for the part of themselves that they were told could not be loved—overcompensating by becoming the most fabulous designer, or decorator, or...writer. Then when the accolades prove just how great they are, unconsciously or not, they've "made-up" for their ugly, shameful side. But there is still inauthenticity to their life, instead of being allowed...to just be—loving and fucking anyone people want to love and fuck.

Well, at this point, I prefer the most authentic stage three. All the fabulousness of the curated, practiced talent, and accomplishments of going after dreams: writing books, traveling the world, along with the shadow side of drugs, overdose, and mental health struggles that were part of the journey, as well. Take it all, or leave it all. *This Is—authentic—Me.*

***

In the spring of 2017, I was on an upswing of healing. I wanted to add a little art therapy into my process. I'd wanted a piece of Scooter's art ever since I laid eyes upon his work. I contacted him and went to his studio to pick out a painting. I ended up with two. I couldn't resist.

Scooter had just completed a series of clown portraitures, some abstractly. The first clown I chose, I saw myself. The face was long like mine. He had a top hat on, which reminded me of a magician's—the first career path I had chosen as a child. Both those attributes drew me to it. Yet it was the background that struck me. It was simply black but very opaque. The clown felt strong, like he had been in the dark, went *through* it, and was on the other side.

It felt like the future me, on the other side of the darkness I was working through. *Never* realizing how much longer it would go on and how much darker it would get, to the point of lights—almost—permanently out. I was sold. That was the clown for me. It was one of the first ones shown, so I continued to look at the rest.

A few paintings later, another piece was revealed. It took my breath away. Another clown. It was much more abstract, yet I saw myself in it too. It didn't look like me at all. It had a more rounded head and square face. It looked as if the pieces of the face were swirling together into place or swirling apart. An identity—two identities—deconstructing and reconstructing, a new mind, heart, and literally head. The transformation stage, where I felt I was at currently, after my father's death and a relationship with death, aspects of myself were deconstructing and reconstructing.

The painting had a melancholy feel, juxtaposed with a bunch of *colors,* bringing forth positivity, a belief in better days ahead once post grief. I thought it was beautiful, that they were both beautiful and meant for me and my healing. Order and chaos, one not being able to exist without the other, reminding me to have great respect for the part each plays. Finding order through chaos became the journey, pushing me to expand my consciousness beyond the other side of chaos to order.

It wasn't until He reconstructed back into my life three years later, that the essence of the second piece of art reminded me of Him, along with the round head and square jaw.

Huh, that's funny, I thought.

***

When it hit me that the Dutch Doctor Amp wanted to introduce me to could be the same man I passed on my street a few months prior, I searched for a picture of the actor Evan Peters on my phone and took a screenshot. The first time I saw Evan Peters on *American Horror Story* when he was in his early twenties, my eyes bulged. The resemblance—except for the eye color—to Him was so similar. All the years I wanted to see His face again, Evan's was the closest I had come. I showed Amp Evan's picture the next time I went into Lollino's and asked if the Dutch Doctor looked like Evan. Amp said yes. I got so excited!

I mean, imagine you're in my wooden shoes—you've heard the story now—experiencing that *first* moment you realize the absolutely *impossible* dream, that you thought for *seventeen* years was *impossible*, was now suddenly *possible*...and at the fingertips of my own neighborhood! After searching the *world!* Yes, I was *beyond* excited! There is no word. A new word would need to be created combining joy, excitement, ecstasy, and bliss...such *happiness* at a dream so close to *potentially* coming true. After the extreme opposite of feelings that had metastasized in my mind and heart after losing Mike, losing myself, wishing for death—and nearly getting it—just *five* months before. I could barely contain my joy!

Yes! The Dutch Doctor is Angel! My intuition screamed. *Life can be like that! Just when you've given up on It, It sends your dream, walking down your street. Believe it!*

I shared with Amp that I thought it could be a man I met many years ago in Amsterdam! Who I considered my first love! Whom I wrote a book about in the hopes I could meet Him again one day! Because I didn't know His name! I shared it all to Amp with the joy that was *erupting* out of me.

It felt so wonderful! Like Mike had sent me Him, a great old friend, sending another old friend from long ago. Well, yes, He didn't know how much of a friend He had been to me all of these years, coming to me in happy and sad times, making appearances; just being there.

But now!

It was here!

The possibility to tell him!

How *incredible!*

We were the *only* two people in the history of the human species—an estimated 108 billion births since the dawn of Homo sapiens—who had *this* experience. I was the only one that could speak to the experience of meeting someone, not asking His name, searching and hoping for *decades*, writing about Him, to now, finding Him. Rather, He found *me!* My street! My café!

And He, He would be the only person who could speak to *His* side of the unconventional experience. Once He learned—of course—that He has been a muse, after a brief time together with essentially a stranger. Whom He meets a lifetime ago, who pops into *His* life twenty years later at the start of a new adventure in a new country, who informs Him that, well, He has been the muse of a writer for three books and a song—at the time—before *Sprookje* and *this writing* was inspired—by Him—as well. Truly, it is two one-of-a-kind-side experiences of the same coin.

I didn't think it would ever happen. I found *acceptance* in a friendship that took the form of a daemon, which I never would have imagined *could* exist as a life experience, nor for a writer when I first dreamt of writing a book twenty-five years before. But it did. The dreams where He appeared throughout the years were always poignant and unexpected visits. Perhaps some people would label Him an imaginary friend.

But He *is* a three-dimensional human too—I didn't have imaginary sex in the darkroom, that I'm certain. He *has* existed *somewhere* on Earth all these years. Now, He potentially had been found in the third dimensional realm of my neighborhood. So, you can imagine, the giggly girlish excitement I felt, and expressed to Amp. The magic of it *electrified* me, including that Amp thought to introduce us. Truly, what were the chances?

As I shared the background with Amp, his eyebrows raised and his face froze. He looked at me like I *was* telling him I had an imaginary friend who was real, and like I *was* a giggly teenage girl—basically, like I was a fool. Amp's expression triggered and brought to the surface the insecurity still unconsciously buried deep inside myself, from long ago at age twenty-seven, *the* feeling that struck a week into the *initial* search, when I hadn't found Him then—that I *was* an *absolute fool* for such an idea.

Amp's look was the complete opposite of Ray's reaction when I shared about Him seventeen years prior in Laguna after the first sighting. Some people see others expressing joy and meet them there, reflect it back to them, and share in it—as Ray did—raising the vibration. Others trigger and reflect the sides of ourselves that we may not want to acknowledge, deal with, or love, that get stuffed down, as with "The Fool" feeling in me. My inner child still felt like a Land of Misfit Toy that didn't know his first love's name, like an *idiot*, because I still held onto *this* particular dream.

It can be lonely and painful doing the shadow work, to get down to those inner wounds, the grains of sand that get lodged in our oysters. Ohhh, they can be so tender to touch. Of *course*, it's easier to disregard and cover them up with layers of nacre. Until, one day, in some unexpected way, they're triggered. My one day, in an unexpected way, was *that* day in Lollino's with Amp, his face reflecting the exact feeling that I didn't want to examine—*was* I a big fool?

I try to keep in mind that the people that trigger me are of no less importance than those that celebrate with me. They are helping me to heal...if I choose to. When I stay aware that feelings ignored, over time, can manifest from the emotional body to the physical in the form of disease. Yes, being triggered, having those feelings rise to the surface to be felt, released, and cleared from the energetic body, is a *positive* thing.

But!

I had not begun my journey with my therapist and certainly was not evolved to that understanding of triggers that morning with Amp. Being triggered *hurt;* experiences that *hurt* were to be avoided—conditioned in us long ago as children, like not touching the stove or sticking our finger in the socket. As soon as I shared the story with Amp, my instinct *screamed* I had said too much. But it was too late.

The feeling of foolishness engulfed me. I was twenty-seven all over again and felt *stupid* for being in this situation, all because I couldn't say hello to a boy in a club. Only now, the feeling was compounded by twenty years behind it and the gut-twisting fact that it happened *again,* because I couldn't say hello to the *same* boy—now a man—on my street. Frozen in a *Groundhog Day*. No compassion for myself or the wounds I had both times.

Even though I learned long ago never to dim my light for someone else's comfort, at that moment, I wished I had with Amp. But I was excited. *The* Mission... was *not* impossible. It was a *massive* moment for me. Regardless of Amp's reaction, I believed the introduction would still happen and, one way or another, I would *at least* learn if the new Dutch Doctor was also Him—Amsterdam Angel—and the same man I passed on my street the 16th of September. I still was not positive, but going on a *strong* gut feeling.

Perhaps the man I saw *was* Angel, but He *was* flight crew, or, simply *not* the Dutch Doctor who Amp wanted to introduce me to. I was guessing at the possibility it was the same man. Even though Amp's confirmation in my Evan Peters description reinforced my intuition, there was still mystery around it.

***

Maybe a week later, I had a dream of Him. We were on a big, gorgeous, sleek white yacht—I was on one end, He was on the other. I was happy to see Him again. But then He vanished before reappearing on another part of the yacht. This went on, again and again, like a whack-a-mole that I didn't want to whack, but reach. Oh, it was frustrating, but so nice to see Him. Maybe, just maybe, it is actually Him coming back in dream too. It was still so *beyond* surreal. My mind was boggled. Completely astonished. Perhaps it is what one calls a miracle? I was certainly beginning to believe in them.

I continued to go into Lollino's, as was always my routine, reading and savoring their delicious coffee. After Amp informed me they were closing the café, I decided to write Him a letter in case the opportunity to travel opened up in the near future. Little did I know how long my health and the pandemic would prevent me from leaving the city.

As you know from reading the play prior to *this* novella, the letter turned into *Sprookje*. The first draft was completed in the first week of December 2020. It was around that same time Sarah—a yoga colleague—invited me to lunch. I was excited yet nervous to share the play with her. Excited to ask for her input because Sarah studied and worked in the theater world, and nervous to share the details of why I had gone MIA from our yoga community.

Sarah was unconditionally loving *and* encouraging. She amped-up *my* excitement with hers that she expressed after hearing the story. She wanted to be a part of the play moving forward and offered to edit it. It was such a lovely surprise. It blew me away and raised my vibration. My desire to continue writing was stoked. I was humbled and grateful to Sarah for the unexpected nudge back onto this familiar road, both in creating this story and writing in general.

I had a positive focus in my life again! It felt *huge* after the darkness of the previous nine months. It was a 180 degree turn from my decision at the end of summer to give up on writing—again—after finishing the third book (I really should count the number of times I have given up). I had shifted into another plan: moving to Amsterdam and starting a business with Art. I didn't see the need to continue writing. I did what I set out to do fourteen years prior and wrote not just one book but three. Writing and I had a good run. I was content with the third book and the ending that came forth.

***

Primarily covering my time in Africa, *The Khat's Mejou* evolved my work from memoir to magical realism. It continued setting up the final fairy tale fourth book.

It was challenging; my first attempt in diverging from memoir.

While *The Khat's Mejou* is based on my life, I was creating a parallel universe. My alternate identity and innocence—Michael—gets separated from me, Anthony, into a parallel universe; caused by a spell cast by Oni in the darkroom on the last night Michael/me and Angel/Him are together at Cockring. But the spell gets cursed and creates a universe where *Michael* is lost in Amsterdam with amnesia always searching for Angel, the only part of his existence he knows. While Anthony and Him go about their respective lives, one traveling the world as a writer and—apparently—the other becoming a doctor.

Michael awakens from a Rip van Winkle-like sleep to search for Angel *only* when Anthony arrives in Amsterdam. Then falls back asleep when Anthony departs. The curse's spell for Anthony is that he only remembers his time in Amsterdam as a recurring dream, searching for a boy. Anthony can't understand why the dreams feel *so familiar*—like *déjà vu*—and decides to write each one down to create a story that, then, turns into books. Michael and Anthony can't exist in Amsterdam at the same time until the spell is broken by finding Angel/Him, at which point Michael and Anthony merge back into one.

I had begun taking out all the Amsterdam visits and searches from the second and third books, referencing them briefly as being dreams. The fourth book would have been all of the Amsterdam visits strung together and told through Michael's eyes under the effects of the spell.

But I figured out a way to finish the series with the third book. It involves the Carnival and the third sighting with Him there in 2013. It is where I ended *The Khat's Mejou*.

Now that I was moving to Amsterdam I was losing interest in completing the series or even putting the third book out. Even more so when the book received an edit from my friend Tom, who indicated areas that needed to be flushed out and reworked. His comments were valid.

It was super challenging, but the idea seduced me to creatively execute a rewrite. Spoiler alert! They were helping Anthony from the other side with the *sprookje* of his life to help evolve their shared soul during its current incarnation… inside Anthony. More imaginary friends, you could say, since one can never have too many.

Ramus, a lion spirit, is one, as well as the narrator. *His* fairy tale is *The Curly Tailed Lion.* He is introduced at the end of the second book, *The Reverie Bubble.* Ramus represents the courageous and confident side of me and brings us both to Cape Town. He's a *ton* of fun!

Oni is a troll-like spirit from a Dutch fairy tale called, *The Oni on His Travels.* Oni represents the side of Anthony that feels ugly for being gay. In casting the spell, Oni's intention was pure. After having only a moment of true love in his own incarnation with the Dutch Prince—who sees his beauty within—just before he dies, Oni only wants to help Anthony and Him have more than a moment of love. Oni knew Anthony felt ugly for being gay—I mean, hello, he is him/me— and senses Anthony would run, which he, I, did. So he casts the spell to bring the part of Anthony that does want love with a man—his innocence, Michael—into existence and to be together with Him/Angel.

But the spell backfires. Oni interferes too much from the other side, according to the laws of the universe and how much a past incarnation of a soul can assist the current. Certain lessons must be overcome and worked out on their own if the soul is to evolve. For "breaking the law" the spell puts the curse on both Anthony and Michael, where they can't exist in Amsterdam simultaneously, and they become lost to one another, until they come into complete vibrational alignment... through radical self-love and *acceptance.*

But Michael is disoriented for many moments in the darkroom from the separation. By the time Michael exits, He/Angel is gone, having left Cockring not long after I/Anthony runs. So Michael never gets to see what He/Angel looks like. Michael only remembers His/Angel's vibration, the frequency of unconditional love. Until Anthony understands and feels *that,* he will not be in alignment and able to merge into one being again with Michael...nor find Him.

You know, that sort of magical realism genre—creating a believable alternate universe that makes sense and is realistic to the reader in how it's told. Sound complicated? It was! I tinkered and kept playing with it on and off for nearly *six* years, since *The Reverie Bubble* came out in 2014.

When Tom pointed out what needed work, I just didn't think I had the energy *or* desire to pursue his suggestions or writing anymore. The *final* book with a big to-do to find *Him* and say, "is this You?" Well, it was appearing like it would never happen. I was moving to Amsterdam, where there would always be the chance to run into Him one day...and if I did, *wonderful.* If not, well, I was starting a new life, and would still keep the promise I made to Him long ago in the pink house.

If there weren't to be a "happy ending/beginning" in the form of writer and muse, meeting in middle age; at *least* I could write it for our lost innocence during the third sighting at the carnival. Before He disappears into the crowd. Before Anthony takes a step toward Him. Angel and Michael *would* reunite, in a parallel universe in front of the Royal Palace. Then disappear into life's carnival, forever young and innocent. Until they find a darkroom, then perhaps, not so innocent.

I *could* be happy with at least Michael and Angel being together. There didn't *need* to be a fourth book. Writing and I were breaking up, amicably, with much love, and a sufficient resolution I could be at peace with for the series, and for my heart. So that's what I wrote. Michael and Angel end up together...happily ever after. The End.

Then, I let go...of the dream of ever seeing Him again.

These were my thoughts...my actions.

Two weeks later, *He* is *walking* down my street, as if He—*poof*—popped out of the pages, and decided to start the *sprookje* again. I will wonder until I take my last breath, *how* that miracle on 19th street...was *possible?*

***

Around the time I finished the first draft of *Sprookje* I began reading Andre Aciman's book *Find Me.* I purchased it during a reading and signing he did at the National Arts Club—where Gloria and I had had *our* moment—in January 2020. I told Mr. Aciman I hadn't read it yet. But it sounded similar to a story I had written about a lover, who I hoped would see the book and come forward because I didn't know his name or how to...*Find Him.*

"Have you thought about putting out an ad?" Mr. Aciman suggested.

In my mind, I laughed a bit when he asked. Mr. Aciman didn't know the extent of the number of years it had been, or that I wasn't even sure if He was from where I met Him.

Where, Mr. Aciman? I thought. *In Amsterdam? Throughout the Netherlands? A personal ad? In the newspaper? Does anybody read personal ads or newspapers anymore? On the internet? Where, Mr. Aciman? Where in the* world *would I put an ad?*

Eleven months later while taking a break from writing, when I began reading *Find Me,* Mr. Aciman's idea popped back into my head. In my neighborhood! Of course! *That's* where I'll put an ad, Mr. Aciman!

Yes, if the new Dutch Doctor *is* really Amsterdam Angel, and He is working in my neighborhood or living in the surrounding area, that is where I'd post ads. Forget social media. An old fashioned ad in the villages and Chelsea. An ad just to Him, that *only* Amsterdam Angel would understand. I allowed myself to get swept up into my own movie, with John Cusack in *Serendipity* as my inspiration. It was worth a shot. Why not?

Yes! My inner 24-year-old hoped He was single and would perhaps be interested in going on a first date. But the 44-year-old I currently was respected the fact that we had not seen each other for nearly twenty years. 44-me tried to keep 24-me *grounded.* Perhaps feelings changed. Perhaps feelings were now unrequited. Perhaps feelings were *never* there. Perhaps He had been a little tipsy; maybe alcohol had Him feeling lovey-dovey when He said, "This is Love"—and didn't *actually* mean love with *me.* I *was* aware of these potential realities. Still, my lost innocence was *found* again, *not* in Amsterdam, but New Amsterdam. Michael re-emerged and was swept up in hope...in romance...in *anything* being possible.

I had my friend, the talented writer Michael Graves—yes, *another* Michael to this story! He has been my personal writing community since I met him and his husband Scott at Ravenwood—Val and Diane's B&B in Provincetown—a few summers in a row, when Dante and I would go to Carnival Week for our anniversary. But more than having writing in common, Michael was just as *big* a believer in love and magic as I. He was excited and supportive of the ad idea, and provided valued input. My mother would be so proud that I was *finally* using my advertising degree.

I decided to get the ads up quickly. Certainly by the 11th of December, the beginning of the "magical" time twenty years prior when I first arrived in Amsterdam—after leaving London—right before meeting Him. Taking *His* lead from long ago, I couldn't think of a more romantic thing to do for someone. If there was the *slightest* bit of truth to Him wondering about *me* over the years—or even *remembering* me—I remained positive that He'd appreciate the intention. I imagined if I were in His wooden shoes...I'd love it.

It helped me to interact even more with the world. It made me happy. I felt positive about life again. For *my* life, my second chance at it, and for love, whether romantic or platonic.

The quickest and easiest ad to create was to take the cover of the original book with His name—or rather the name I gave Him—and the title of the book *Amsterdam Angel* already read like the salutation of a brief letter to Him. I did three versions of it. Since the ad was only for one Dutch man's eyes, I put the message in His language.

Underneath *Amsterdam Angel* on the first ad, I put, *Wie ben jij?* (Who are you?), followed by His infamous question, *Weet je wat dit is?* (Do you know what this is?). On the second ad, *Is het jou?* (Is it you?), with His infamous answer, *Dit is liefde* (This is love) afterward. Finally, the third ad read, *Waar ben jij?* (Where are you?), with, *Twintig Jaren!* (Twenty years!), following it. Since He didn't know me by the name on the bottom of the book, I covered it up with a heart followed by the name I had given him—Michael—and my website at the bottom. I was happy with it!

I printed them up and started late one night on the 11th of December. It was the anniversary of my father's death. I hoped his spirit would come along. I taped them to lampposts, phone booths, and various other places well into the early morning of the 12th—my date for releasing projects into the third dimension. This time instead of a book, it was an ad—thanks for the idea, Mr. Aciman—posted around the villages and Chelsea. I made sure to place some around the hospitals and medical centers, which made me realize what a daunting task I was undertaking as there were so *many* medical facilities in this part of New York City.

How would I *ever* know at which one He worked? He could be *anywhere*. I randomly guessed where to tape them, imagining Him on a walk to work or just a walk around the city. The possibilities seemed *endless*, like a Yayoi Kusama infinity room. I felt so very close to Him, being on the same island. Being *pretty* sure anyway, that after twenty years we were *both* on the same tiny island. Yet I also felt so very far away from Him. How, on an island of *millions*, would I *Find Him?* I had to try.

I went out and put more ads up the following night. Sunday morning, I noticed that the city had already taken some down. It didn't discourage me. Many remained up. Plus, I was still riding high on *just* the possibility a dream could come true. John Cusack—*the* grand marshal in 80's movies for displays of love—was in da house as my spirit mentor. *He* didn't give up. I allowed myself to believe in holiday magic again, which I hadn't done since my father's death four years prior. It made my heart feel light again and...*thrilled!*

I was healing. I was trying. Trying to *live.* Feeling creative. Feeling joy. Standing up and starting again...rising *up.* Where just a few months prior, I felt *none* of that.

The thought of the simple dream: to say "thank you" to a boy—now a man—filled me with such bliss! It was an extraordinarily natural high knowing there was a possibility to share how our encounter had been so much more special than He or I could *ever* imagine, inspiring nearly my *entire* body of work. Our *brief* experience providing me with...a *career!* One that I *never* could have comprehended twenty-five years earlier at nineteen, sitting in Jennifer—*that* teacher—Dawson's creative writing class at Michigan State University, the semester Mike and I met and pledged Phi Kappa Psi. Jennifer's *passion* for writing sparked me, ignited my dream to write a book, and sent me falling down an *Anthony in Wonderland—sprookje*—rabbit hole that led...to *this.*

The thought of Him throughout the years—in dreams, in sightings—made me want to be a better person, to reflect on what I needed to in myself. How could anybody ask for anything more out of a relationship, platonic or romantic, imaginary or real—whatever that means at this point—with someone else? My heart and mind had rocketed out of a coma, out of the ICU, because of His IC, through presence...or the seemingly *strong* possibility of it.

***

After the weekend that the ads went up—the 14h of December to be exact—I continued with the break from writing and switched creative gears again. I wanted to create art in another way, through abstract photography. The creativity was percolating. I was inspired that afternoon to play with a cover idea for the playbill and poster for *Sprookje.*

Back in 2006 when I wrote the first book, the original idea I envisioned, as the cover for *Amsterdam Angel* was a blonde-haired, blue-eyed man wearing a blue knit cap. His eyes would be like the ocean—when a bright sunny day shines upon the water and makes it sparkle—crystalized like blue topaz as I remembered His, the moment in Cockring when I came out of the dark, into the light of His eyes.

I began by using the picture of Evan Peters on my phone that I'd shown to Amp. I played with the shading to make it more abstract. I wanted to lose the

143

distinction of Evan's face and see if I could get it looking more like Him. I worked and worked on it for a while. But I just couldn't get it to where I wanted. It was still looking too much like Evan. So I took a break.

It was fun, a different creative outlet from writing for the day. But I was a long way off from creating the playbill. I threw my computer and book in a bag, put on my coat and shoes, to head to an East Village café, as had become my routine by that time.

Ahhhhhh, I thought as I approached my building's front door. *If I could just see* His *face, instead of staring at Evan's for so long!*

As soon as I opened the door to my building it was as if a gust of energy blasted me back and my eyebrows raised. There, at my *doorstep*, passing right by me was an elderly lady and *Him!* Black knit cap, black facemask, black trench coat, jeans, and trainers—or...was it Evan Peters? I was staring at Evan's picture so long it was as if Evan's face superimposed on the man now in front of me who looked like the man I passed on my street three months earlier, who *both* looked like...*Him*... Amsterdam Angel!

Whoever it was, He shot me a side glare the instant I opened the door and He noticed me. It was as if ice daggers flew out of His eyes, hit me, and knocked me backward, along with the *shock* that He, was now at my *doorstep*. Or was it Evan Peters? Living in New York City long enough you realize that usually when you think you see a celebrity and wonder if it is indeed them, it is very likely that it is, because, well, you're in New York City and many are there.

But *who* was the elderly lady, Evan's grandmother? The hat and the mask were so concealing I wasn't sure. Him? Or Evan? I had to get a better look. When I stepped on the sidewalk behind Him—or Evan—and the lady, they were arm and arm. He—or Evan—immediately began slowly sliding his hand down her arm and grabbed her hand. I had a flashback to when I did the same to His in the darkroom all those years ago...with gentleness.

The energy felt closed off to me. It didn't feel welcoming. I walked to the other side of the street. I hoped they would turn south at the end of the block and cross 19th street. Then I could get a *good* look at Him, or Evan, as we passed each other head on. I had to know if it was Him—after *all* the years. But they turned the other way and went north up 9th Avenue.

Ugh! I thought.

Triggers of the initial search and taking second looks came back. Feelings of being a fool came back. I crossed the street to go north, as well, to the nearest bike station. This was ridiculous! *Was* Amsterdam Angel and the new Dutch Doctor the same person...or not? Give me a break universe! Jeeeeezzz. I was still in a state of shock, absolutely *stunned* that this was possible—that it could really be Him.

At the next block they turned and crossed the bike lane, before pausing at the island for traffic. I continued north to grab a bike. As I passed, I tried to get another look. When I did, He—or Evan—turned their head and gave me a second look. *Finally* I get a second look from Him.

But!

It came with *another* round of ice daggers. Yes, they were *definitely* meant for *me!* Woooo Wheee! Jeeeeezzzz! In my family we call that the van Leeuwen glare. Ahhhh, if He only realized how *amazing* I am, how kind and fun...and funny! And! And! And! That I dreamt of Him literally and figuratively, that He had been a best friend, supporting and being there through the years. And that He was a muse. If He only knew *all* that *and* decided to marry me...He would fit right into my family with an ice dagger glare like that! Jeeezzzzz! Brrrrrrr! Ahhhh *Kom op!* (Come on!) Universe! Give! Me! A! Break!

But my ego still wanted to doubt that the impossible was possible. Hoping for years had worn on my mind. Celebrities also give that same icy glare sometimes—when you're trying to figure out if it's them, and you stare a bit too long—that says, "*Yeah it's me! Don't bother me!*" Whoever it was the eyes said it all, "*Don't bother me!*" So I didn't.

I grabbed a bike, went to the East Village, then *straight* to my therapist two days later. I blabbed the entire twenty-year story to her like a balloon flying through the air deflating, with only a few minutes left for her to get a word in.

"I think it's really Him!" I said. "The *same* guy from the darkroom! *Twenty* years ago! It's *incredible* to me! The odds! It's absolute magic! I can't *imagine* what could be more of a *miracle* than *this*! *How* did he come to be in my neighborhood! Go to my café! The odds are like winning the lotto! And this has been my lotto dream! And...He's *mad* at me? Three books! A play! A song! The search! Thousands of dollars spent, the writing, the editing, the *therapy*—including now *this* session adding to it, and probably more, because of this latest development—trying to figure out why? Why, even when I let Him go, He comes back in *some* way! All of *that!* Over *twenty years!* Now, He's in my neighborhood...and he's *mad* at me? I just can't believe it!"

Of *course* I could understand! He didn't know *any* of that. All He knew was that I walked by Him, twice, twenty years apart.

But jeeezzz, I'm sorry I walked by. Give me a break Beautiful Man from the Dark! It's been twenty years! You were all bundled up back then! I was on mushrooms and ecstasy! (Wow that's a combination!) We were in the dark for, I don't know, a couple of hours? The light was bright afterward! Your light was so bright! Ahhhh, give me a break Beautiful Man from the Dark!

A small part of me thought I was hallucinating again.

Maybe it was Evan Peters and his grandmother.

Maybe the new Dutch Doctor was still Him.

Or maybe it wasn't.

I was still completely bewildered that it *could* be Him. A twenty years search, and now He appears on my street *twice* within a matter of a few months. But I carried on with the positive outlook that the Dutch Doctor was Him, and that the ice daggers came from Evan. Be optimistic! *He's* not mad at me! Evan Peters was! Yes, that's a more positive outlook.

Christmas Eve and Christmas night more ads went up. I figured, why not? Give it a double effort. It was funny how the YouTube rabbit hole comes in. I was Googling the idea of serendipity from the moment it felt like I was beginning to live the film. I began seeing the word "Amsterdam" and "Angel" all around me—sometimes one right after the other. And blue knit caps! It seemed blue was the "it" color of the winter season for caps. Guys *everywhere* in blue knit caps; some with blond hair, blue eyes, and a certain age. On bikes, on the street, in cafes, everywhere! It was like a scene from *Amsterdam Angel, The Musical,* where thirty blond hair, blue-eyed "Angels" in blue knit caps come at me and pass me in every direction, walking, running, on bikes—Amsterdam Angels *everywhere* as a song and dance number ensues!

As whiplashing and bonkers as it felt I kept venturing out. There was a chance, that a rare dream could come true. And to increase my chances of that happening, I would *have* to rejoin the world again. *Engage* with it, with life. Push through any PTSD triggers. Him/The Muse/Angel/The Dutch Doctor, through absolutely *no* conscious effort on His part, was inspiring me to be kinder to myself, and continue to rise up.

***

As the New Year began, so did my meditation routine. 2021 definitely needed a calmer mind. I launched into a ten-week series from The Star that provided focused intentions and visualizations. One started with The Star instructing a visualization starting at my feet and going up—imagining my body going off like a sparkler as I did. I thought it was an intriguing way to use my imagination and got into it. Beginning with the darkness at my feet, I could see the sparkles lighting them up in the dark, moving up to my shins, then up to my knees. Once to my knees, *His* face popped in at knee hieght. He wore the blue knit cap and smiled like at Cockring twenty years prior. *His* eyes were sparkling too. He spooked me! Not in a way that made me afraid. Simply surprised, like at my doorstep...and *why*, why is He now in my meditation?

Where did You come from?

A few days later, again, He popped in. This time the silhouette of His face floated from the top right down to the bottom left.

What are you doing here? Who are You mysterious Dutch man who has come into my life again? 3D realm, dreams, inspiration, and now meditations! Who are *You?*

A couple weeks into the New Year, I was walking down my street returning home when I saw Isabella coming toward me. She had made many of my coffees— always with the brightest Brazilian smile—at Lollino's. I hadn't seen much of her since Lollino's had closed their doors. Moments before we approached each other, it dawned on me.

Isabella! I don't know why I didn't think to ask her! Maybe she made the Dutch Doctor's coffee and had a chat with Him. Maybe she knows his name! I thought.

As she approached me, the same big, beautiful smile she always greeted me with at the café came shining back. I returned it with my own. We caught up a bit before I asked her if she remembered the Dutch Doctor and if she ever got his name.

"No, but Amp got His information," she said.

That was *certainly* not a direction I expected the question to go.

"*What?*" I responded, a little shocked as my heart sank. "Amp told me he didn't get it."

"Oh...maybe he didn't. I thought he did."

"Okay, well, do you remember what He looked like?" I pulled out Evan Peter's picture that I still had on my phone. "Was it like this?" I said as I showed her Evan's picture.

"No."

"*No?*"

"His face was longer, I think, about your height, maybe taller," she added.

"My height? Maybe taller? Than me?"

"I don't know. I don't remember."

As we parted ways, I was more confused than ever, and a bit sad. I was confused because Isabella's description was not the same as Amp's. Maybe, the Dutch Doctor *wasn't* Angel. Maybe, the man from a month earlier at my doorstep *was* Evan Peters. Maybe, the Dutch Doctor and the man at my doorstep were the same and *was* Angel. Maybe, the man I passed on the street was Angel but not the Dutch Doctor, and not the man at my doorstep. Jeeezzz. Confusing, right?

I was sad because Isabella seemed so sure when she had first relayed that Amp did get the Dutch Doctor's information. Maybe she *was* mistaken. I gave her the benefit of the doubt, of course. But if she was right, and Amp did get the doc's details, then Amp wasn't honest with me...but why?

My insecurity immediately made me wonder if Amp might have told the Dutch Doctor everything I told him a couple months before. And that the Dutch Doctor *was* Angel who connected the words that it was I, Michael—to Him— Anthony to *you*. Then rejected Amp's offer to introduce us. Because He *was* mad at me for walking by in September. Possibly he even asked Amp not to give me *any* information about Him. Or, perhaps Amp didn't want to get involved with what sounded like, I don't know, one of those situations people don't want to get involved in, with two people that were...involved, at one point.

My heart started to crack at the thought that Dr. Angel rejected me, was angry or hurt, or both for being walked by. Ohhhh, if He only knew! What *you* all know from *Sprookje*. My heart cracked at the thought that it might have been Angel... at my doorstep! And the ice daggers out of His eyes *were* meant for me. Man, talk about The Promise! I sure added to my promise list with *Him* that day, that if He *ever* did want to be friends in the 3rd dimensional world, I would surely promise *never! Never* to do *anything* to generate *that* look again out of His eyes...to *mij!* (me!)

Please! Brrrrrrrr! Ouch!

My heart cracked, too, at the thought that I had been deceived. Could I feel hurt to think that Amp had potentially lied to me? Yes, absolutely! Nobody needs to make themselves the guardian of my feelings. *Whatever* the truth may be. If the truth was that it is Angel and He didn't want anything to do with me, so be it. I'd deal with it and let go.

Yes, I could honor the hurt if Amp lied for whatever reason; feel it, forgive, and move on. Absolutely. And if the truth was that Amp just didn't want to get involved, then say that. Either way, could a lie that no information was received just be easier? Sure. I suppose so.

Had I ever lied in forty-five years because I made myself the guardian of someone else's feelings, because I felt I needed to "protect" them, or because it was easier than getting involved in something? I'm sure I probably have, yes. This doesn't mean I haven't been truthful the majority of my life, so I gave the same benefit of the doubt to Amp. We're all everything at one point. In my logical mind, I could forgive Amp if he lied. But there was nothing I could do.

Perhaps Isabella was wrong. Perhaps there was still a chance. But not long after I ran into Isabella I had a dream of Amp. He was staring at me with a sorrowful look.

Ahhh jeeezzz, am I picking up on some telepathic remorse vibration from Amp? Did Isabella tell him I ran into her and asked about the Dutch Doctor? Ugh, perhaps I have to face the timeline that the Dutch Doctor is Him *and that He doesn't want* anything *to do with me...ever!*

What was I to do with the play? It was healing for me, yes, that was my priority. But it was also a letter for Him and was in Sarah's hands being edited. Could I respect His wishes that He *may* not want to be found...by *me* specifically... *if* indeed He was the Dutch Doctor? Ohhhh, how could I know what His wishes were? I wasn't even *positive* if it was the same person! Just a gut feeling; making up a scenario as if it were Him, because if it was, and those ice daggers the previous month were for me, ahhhh, I wouldn't want to do *anything* to trigger a bad memory for Him. Was that what I was to Him...a bad memory? When He was this inspiring imaginary friend and muse for years to me? What to do? What to do!

Give up on the writing...*again*...like had been the plan just months before as I prepared to move to Amsterdam? I'd done it many times before. But never with the awareness that He potentially knew about me, where I lived, and *perhaps* didn't want anything to do with me. So *this* time in giving up, letting go of the writing, I was letting go of the muse. Letting go of the muse, I was letting go of Him. Letting go of Him, I was letting go...of the dream. Was it time to let go...of it *all*? I brought that question into my next meditation.

I was still fairly green to meditation. I didn't know what, if anything, I would experience or how to *get* an answer to my question. A feeling? A knowing? I didn't have a clue. I simply went within, concentrated on my breathing, and pondered the question. What came to me, to my surprise, was an image. Outer space. Him. Me. Spinning. We were connected by one hand holding onto the other. Spinning faster and faster. Until gradually the force began to pull us apart as we continued spinning in the orbit we had created. Still with our hands outstretched to the other.

Ah, time to let go, I thought. *How much more literal could it be?*

But then in an instant, like two magnets, our hands were sucked back into one another. We held on, stronger, and began spinning, *faster*. I didn't understand why, why *this* particular vision of us came through in my meditation and more importantly what did it mean...don't let go?

Ahhhh, who are You?

With the new information from Isabella, I thought back to His eyes that day, the glare, twice! They were *angry* eyes. It reminded me of Dr. Phil—yes—Dr. Phil. It was a period in my relationship with Dante when we were arguing a lot, not being able to see the other's side, or even listening to it, only wanting to have our side heard or validated, and it usually escalated to anger.

I received an epiphany from Dr. Phil one day. I caught his words on anger. He said anger was nothing more than the outward manifestation of pain. Bingo Phil! Thank you! Game changer. From then on, every time Dante and I began escalating to arguing, I tried to curtail it quickly as Phil's words popped into my head. We were both in emotional or mental pain in some way. I certainly don't want someone I love to be in pain. So it helped to de-escalate the situation. Thanks, Philly!

I remembered His eyes from that day. I was still a bit chilly from the ice daggers—that on the surface were anger—shooting at me. Dr. Phil's words came back with the recollection and I felt pain behind them too. I can't speak for Him, of course. But I felt pain. He was hurt. And I could *absolutely* understand that.

Oh my, ohhhhhhhh myyyyyyyy, how our experiences were so very different.

My experience—quite simply—a *best* friend, going back *many* years, with wonderful times together. Even if the majority of those times are His visits in my dreams.

His experience of me—most likely—briefer: a stranger in the night from many years ago, who apparently lived in New York City and walked right by Him—twice—twenty years apart. Hurtful, I can imagine...yes! That's, I think, a fairly good guess of His experience of me. *Maybe* we could add to that: I'm a good kisser and hot sex. But we would have to clarify with Him on *that.*

Our experiences couldn't be more opposite. Perhaps He thought of me over the years, perhaps not. I doubt. Highly. He searched, wrote, hoped, and longed for years to meet *me* again. One thing our experiences probably have in common is disappointment; a tortured misunderstanding that could be rectified with...a "hello."

As the bundled up, masked man with the elderly lady—perhaps not Evan Peter's grandmother, but a patient of the Doc's out for a walk—at my doorstep replayed in my mind, the eye's that said, "I'm hurt", also strengthened my intuition. That! After *twenty* years of attempting the impossible...the impossible was accomplished, and the man at my doorstep was not Evan Peters but, in fact, ladies, gentlemen, and them...*the* Amsterdam Angel himself!

He had been found!

Hallelujah!

He *had* been found!

On my doorstep!

Though, He certainly was *not* falling at it, as the saying goes.

Un!

Be!

Lieve!

A!

Ble!

On the one hand I was *absolutely, positively, completely* O! Ver! Joyed! As those of you who have followed this story for a decade since *Amsterdam Angel* came out could imagine. Now, double that times to *two* decades, and imagine going on the search, writing books, and you can more deeply empathize my joy that He had been *found!* He'd *actually* been found. And the irony of it all, was that He "found" me—as if Mr. Aciman foreshadowed it, sent Him a message...*Find* Me. Well, He did! On my street...twice! And the second time at my doorstep! Are you kidding me?

How. Is. That. Possible?

On the other side of that coin, I was *so* very sad to think that He was hurt. And that I was the cause of it...again! Twenty-years later! Even knowing the demons that gave me a one-two knockout punch that summer day, as I walked by. It still felt like I hurt my buddy, my muse, my best friend, twice! Yes! It cloaked me with sadness. It doubled the weight of the regret of the last life, and the bittersweetness of the entire twenty-year experience.

***

There was nothing I could do but carry on with my healing and therapy and reading, and learning. By February Sarah completed the first edit. Again she blew me away with the elation she expressed for the story and her desire to continue to be a part of it. The energy that came forth from her expression blasted me like a Care Bear belly with such encouragement from a trained theater person to a first time…"play writer?"

Is that what I was now, was my newly chosen "label" of an entrepreneur in Amsterdam…switching? I didn't know. I tried to remain open, flexible, and remember, that life can take a dream and expand it beyond anything I could ever imagine…it had before. Since I couldn't pursue the latter because of the pandemic preventing entrance into the Netherlands, I decided to carry on with the former in the interim.

Yes, I would continue with the story that from the beginning was meant to… *Find Him.* Even though, He was mad at me; and perhaps could care less about His given label by me of…The Muse. Maybe I can only speak for myself, but *I'd* like to know if I was a muse to some stranger I met twenty years ago. *I'd* like to know what that life experience is like. But only one person on the planet could speak to that…*my* muse…Him. And He wasn't speaking to me. I was in the *doghouse* with my muse, who popped back into my life, now three-dimensionally. How am *I* having *this* life experience?

Not only was He upset with me, He now knew I lived on 19th street and would probably avoid it—and me—like a pandemic virus. So no more running into Him there! And still, no clue where He could be working. There was *nothing* I could do to rectify what felt like a big misunderstanding. It felt like I was trapped. Unable to be heard from the other side of a carnival funhouse mirror—only not so fun—and He was right *there.* But He couldn't see me *or* hear me.

***

Come mid-February, I did see Him. Not in the 3D world but in another dream. We met at a restaurant in the city. It was our first meeting. We were both so happy to see each other and greeted one another with big smiles and a hug near the bar. It felt like electricity between us again, but respectful. We held no assumptions that since it had been sexual and romantic twenty years ago, we'd begin from there again. Nevertheless the sparks were charged. I welcomed Him to New York City, and we talked about 9/11 and The Statue of Liberty—which felt like a bit more confirmation to my gut He is in NYC. It was the type of conversation people do with a smile the whole time because it feels like you're tickling one another with your energies, and you can't help but smile as you attempt to speak.

We sat down with a group of people. I didn't know who they were in the dream. We both wanted to sit next to each other. One man across from us, for some reason, took his shirt off. Sure, the man had a nice body. I caught Him check the man out, along with a flirt in the eye the man sent His way.

The dream reflected and brought to the surface an insecurity to be healed—that He had eyes for someone else. A bit of the hope that He wanted to have eyes only for me was dashed. I excused myself and went to the bar to let Him be free to explore the shirtless possibility. I had a couple vodka drinks, which is not like me. But I did, before returning to the table.

"Where did you go?" He asked in a way that revealed He'd been wondering and waiting.

"Just to have a drink," I said before slipping back into the group.

When I awoke, I was both excited and frustrated. Excited to see Him again and frustrated because, well, enough of the dreams already! 3D please!

***

At the beginning of March I had my ketamine session with my therapist. I had ordered Gloria's book weeks before. I wanted to remember how she put into words the 'moment of love' in case it rekindled something in me with what I was expressing with *Sprookje*. I went to Café Flor early that morning and began re-reading it before my session.

When I lied on my therapist's couch that afternoon and my pharmacologist began the injections, I really had no clue what to expect. They said it was really like no other drug to compare it to. Maybe mushrooms as a distant cousin. OK, so I was going on a "trip" somewhere. I'd heard a bit about the "oneness" feeling it provided, with no separation from you, from him, from her, from them, from… me. That we-are-all-one type of Kumbaya feeling…Om! A bit of a death of ego experience in order to get there…that would be nice. We could all use a bit of death to our ego from time to time.

As I began dropping inward, it felt a bit like the sunken place from Get Out—sinking deeper and deeper into the couch—but without the scary side. Instead I felt cozy, and safe. On the floating journey, down out of my conscious mind and into my subconscious, I saw Gloria. I began relaying the Gloria story to the ladies. As I did, a piece of it dawned on me that I had forgotten.

At some point when I began writing *Sprookje,* Gloria's idea from fifteen years prior, had already began to bubble back up when I was going to the East Village every day to work on the play. I would hop on a Citi Bike at 20th and 8th Avenue, ride east until I hit 2nd Avenue, then head south toward Tompkins Square Park. I don't know at what point I realized it, but the route took me through Gramercy Park, past The National Arts Club, where I remembered Gloria, and our moment of love. From that point on, each day that I passed the club, I gave a little salute and shout out to Gloria.

"I love you Gloria! Thanks for being my guardian Angel of love! Now let's find Him!"

I didn't know what was coming over me. Love, falling in love again, with Him? With myself? With life? With Gloria? (Well, who wouldn't fall in love with Gloria). Who *cares*! It felt good. No! It felt *great* to embrace the lost innocence of love again, and romance with any or all of the above. It was certainly healthier than months before. Being high on crystal meth, needing to fuck to feel *something*, to feel *anything* besides pain, and to fuck the pain away. Yes, I think anyone would agree it was *much* healthier to embrace the possibility of a second chance with first love.

Shortly after I remembered and shared about Gloria, it was as if I took off flying. Soaring like a hawk, which I'd seen that day in Central Park on my way to the session—a spirit animal to guide me to see a higher perspective. The 'flight' took me through visuals of landscapes of all types of nature, and even The Great Wall.

The second injection felt like being tucked into the coils and tunnels of the brain. It was coral in color and quite snug, cozy but slightly constricting. I felt I was in a tight rubber suit with entities of the light—like fairies—around me. Three, maybe four of them were pulling, tugging and squeezing me out of my rubber suit, out of my ego. It was my death of ego moment. Afterward, everything did feel like one, no separation, a dissociation from the mind into the soul, the "remembrance" through feeling the eternal being I am in the temporary costume of a human. It took a minute. I felt the fairies laughing while they tugged at the suit. I must have had a sticky ego that wouldn't let go.

The first two doses served as a way to ease into the experience. The third and final injection, my therapist said might feel as if I just *take off!* Man, she wasn't kidding. I took off like a rocket as Earth became smaller and smaller, and in an instant, I was in outer space looking down at the planet.

It began tilting from North America to South America and I saw Brazil. Then the Earth tilted back north toward Iceland. Then a visual of flying with a frequency I *felt* was His coming in as we zoomed in from space to an Icelandic landscape. We were flying through an icy gorge with a river running through it. Both the water and the gorge had stunning shades of icy blues.

Then in an instant I was sucked back into outer space. All of the planets lined up like a set of croquet balls. A giant croquet stick flew down and knocked the planets around this way and that way in all directions of the cosmos, with the echoed sounds of my therapist and my pharmacologist's frequencies as I described what was happening.

As the planets went scattering about, I dropped *deeper* within. I was in the dark, *somewhere,* waiting to see where and wondering what would happen next. As if reaching the curtain onstage in a dark theater, placing my hand upon it to reveal what was on...the other side.

It was a peaceful, serene forest. Astonishingly enchanting. Pine trees of all widths and heights, pine needles and moss covering the ground. Rays of sunlight were peeking through the branches and giving the forest sparkle. Serenity. I felt so safe.

After all that I had endured in those last few months, last several years, last forty-four years on Earth, I felt safe not only in my body, but in the galaxy. I had a spot in it. I was a part of it all, of energy, of frequencies playing out with the vision of a shimmering forest in shades of green and brown, an avatar world. The vibration was less dense than the third dimension, perhaps fifth. I gently moved forward, slowly taking in every part of the forest, and *explored.* The frequency of peace hummed, of simply *being.* I went *home.*

Then!

He popped in!

His face came poking out from around a tree in a peek-a-boo way.

Gloria was in my thoughts, my conscious mind, as I slowly dropped into my subconscious and could still talk. There were no visuals of her. Perhaps because I had begun reading Gloria's book that day, she was on my mind. Regardless it reminded me of the shout out I did to her and the excitement I felt for life again during that time.

But He! He seemed to just *be* there already, in my sub-conscious, waiting for me to find Him...within. I had dropped into a dimension where I couldn't speak to the ladies anymore about what was happening. They were not there in the forest. I was not *there*...in Manhattan, on 72nd St., in my therapist's office. I was on a vision quest, in a forest *within* me. Deep within and, He was there. I could *see* Him, and He could see me, as our seemingly eternal dance of hide-and-go-seek and peek-a-boo resumed.

He wore a green pullover that blended with the shades of the green forest, yet it was His eyes that stood out. They were crystalized, a beautiful shining blue topaz color. Along with His smile, both happy to see me and pleased that He surprised me. That was it, just a pop in before He nudged me in thought through telepathy. Telling me to *keep moving forward, keep moving forward* through the forest, amongst the trees and through them.

In the distance I could see a stream. Beyond that it was as if a field of blue topaz crystals matching His eyes stretched in the distance and were sparkling radiantly. I walked toward the stream to walk along it, going with its flow. The wisdom I learned from my time in Africa pulsated: life is a river; we must go with its flow.

However, before I began the walk along the river, I dropped again, deeper within my sub-conscious. I was shot further down or up or sideways or whatever way consciousness was flowing me at that point. So I went with it. "I" don't think I had a choice.

I found myself back in outer space, with Him, a "third" person view of Us. It was the end of time. The light, *the* light—Source Itself—that *every* soul and all creation came from—was off to the left, waiting for Us. Every other soul of *all* time had returned to It. Home.

He and I were still creating. At that dimension whatever one goes to before merging back into Source, 11th, 12th, who knows. I don't. This dimensionality stuff was still new to me.

Whichever it was, the forms that we took were just two heads, floating through space. In Our wake was nothingness, a black canvas of the cosmos. Ahead of Us, were beautiful landscapes of color and nature coming from Our thoughts. It was Our co-creation from Our combined consciousness. Flowing out of Us. His floating head then turned to my floating head.

"Incredible isn't it?" He said with a smile at what we were creating.

I looked at Him, smiled, and nodded. But at the same time felt slight pressure from Source.

"Come on you two! Get your heads over here! You're the last ones! Merge with us *all* again into ONE! It's been *forever*—literally—since we were all together! We'll start it all over again. I promise!" Source said.

He and I looked at each other like We knew it was time to go home. But We were going to take just a bit more time. Then resumed floating together creating stunning landscapes from Our united consciousness, before I returned to a visual of flying again through landscapes and a first-person perspective as I began "coming back" from my internal vision quest.

Now, what are You doing in my ketamine session? And why do we get along so well creating landscapes in the 11th dimension, playing hide-and-go-seek in the forest of the 5th, but in the 3rd I get ice daggers? Huh? What's up Doc...with that? But as always, nice to see You...again...in whatever form or dimension You want to meet up in. OK, I get it. We're multi-dimensional beings having multi-dimensional experiences. But could I get a 3D one please Meneer Mooie Man? (Mr. Beautiful Man?) Come on; let's hug it out there!

Regardless, the session gave me that feeling of utter safety in life after the politics and protests and pandemic and loss and drugs and near death. I felt so very safe in the world again, in my body. It was a wise decision to do drugs again.

***

A couple of weeks later I was in the Hamptons dog-sitting Lilly for Liza. Liza encouraged me to explore some of the hiking trails that are scattered throughout the area. I had always gravitated toward the beach because of the ticks. But it was still off-season for ticks, so I did a different hike each day. Gradually as the hikes went on each had an element of the vision of the forest from my ketamine session.

Huh, that's funny, I thought.

Until one forest was *the* vision. It had the same type of trees and moss on the ground, the same shades of green and brown, with sunlight peeking through. How is *that* possible? A premonition in my ketamine session of a forest I was soon to be led to? But why? What was happening? It was incredibly surreal.

Toward the end of my time in the Hamptons, I was coming back from Montauk after doing a hike called Amsterdam. Along the way, I pulled off the road at a second hiking spot. Again there were pine trees. I made my way through them to the dunes. Once I climbed the sand, at the top of the dune, the ocean stretched before me. The sunlight was catching it just right to make the water shimmer, like thousands of sparkling blue crystals. I thought from the ketamine journey it was a field of blue crystals beyond the forest, but perhaps it was the ocean, this ocean?

"What is happening?" I asked my therapist. "How did that happen? It's not a coincidence. How did the vision inside me, appear in my reality weeks later. I don't understand. It's magic to me and I don't understand."

"Don't ask how, or try to understand, just allow," she advised.

Just allow.

OK.

Upon my return to the city, I awoke to a feeling or a realization, that He could have met someone by that point. Maybe it was my ego trying to keep me safe. Direct me away from thinking I had a chance, in that way at least. Stay realistic. Start with a hello. Keep myself open to others as well. But, ahhhhhh, I try to let go and it's like a revolving door, then He appears in other dimensions or dreams, or in person, and I'm pulled back in. It was beginning to seem futile though. How would I possibly *Find Him*, and, if I did, and it was Him, are there more ice daggers waiting for me?

It was a Sunday afternoon when I decided to get outside for a walk. Shortly after I did it began to rain. I turned down the next block to circle back home. There was a medical facility on the street. I was on the opposite side of the street as I approached it. Scaffolding surrounded a building ahead of me. It had a sign above with the company name of the contractors working on the home: Dutchman.

Yes of course. How could I not think of Him as I looked at the sign above my head? He is a Dutch man. Then I looked across the street at the medical facility.

Huh, I wondered. *Could* that *be the one? Could that actually be where He, the new Dutch Doctor has been going, every day for the last several months...in my neighborhood?*

It was a fairly good guess—with a fairly clear, literal—sign, along with a gut feeling.

***

In April, He appeared in dream—twice—the nights before and after the first anniversary of Mike's death. I was visiting sweet Elodie, who was turning three in Kentucky. In the first dream my energy was floating through The Cape, down Route 6 toward Provincetown, when He appeared in the sand along the side of the road. He was hitchhiking. He looked and shined like He did that day in September on my street, healthy, happy, confident, smiling, and looking for a ride to P-town. His energy had the feel of an adventurer, present, palpable...a turn-on. And in some reality, that's what happened. My brakes slammed and my tires screeched to pick up that hot hitchhiker—for life—before another P-town bound boy got to Him; reunion on Route 6. He wore confidence well, very sexy.

Yes! My heart felt peaceful when I woke in my niece's bed. Not because I had a good night sleep because sweet Elodie gave up her bed for me; or because Elsa, Anna, and that silly Olaf were smiling at me from the sheets—although those facts *were* a bonus. It felt peaceful to see Him, smiling at me, happy, and ready for an adventure. But more poignantly because His appearance was perfectly timed for that day, as my thoughts drifted back to a year prior, to the news that I would receive about Mike. Felt like my thoughtful old friend, remembering a tender time and showing up to comfort me with His presence...and a smile.

In the next night's dream, we were having dinner at a restaurant. It was the first date, with all the nerves of a first date to accompany it for us both. He looked slightly unhealthy. I didn't imagine He could be. Maybe He was; who knows.

I took it more as a reflection of where I felt my health was currently at—still not quite confidence-worthy. Perhaps His nervousness reflected my unconscious insecurity about both this and dating at that point, which was bubbling to the surface to feel and heal with self-love.

What would I share about the previous year with Him, or any other sexy man I went on a date with? I hadn't reached a confident state of complete, radical self-acceptance of what I had done to myself. To be able to share it without shame. I hadn't embraced or understood it as my proudest accomplishment in life, making me feel stronger in mind and heart because of it. I was the only person that could know what it took to pull myself out of that.

Nor did I embrace the perspective that the *right* person for me would understand life and the difficulties it throws; *that* person would *see* me. He would feel my energy, feel good around it, and go with their heart instead of any label the head could give. Anyone that didn't was best to fade away...right away. Being honest right from the start with no shame would save me and the other person precious time.

Yet in the dream, He was smiling, and seemed *happy* to be there as we conversed. It felt really wonderful, of course. I mean, hello, I had waited twenty years for a date. Now I was on one, in the dream world anyway. We seemed to get along so well there.

Why do we get along so well in the dream world, Doc?

A couple of weeks later, I was in California for some business. I visited Laguna Beach and picked up a tea at the Koffee Klatch. Then walked down the street of the first sighting of Him so long ago—that started it *all*. Near *the* spot, there was a flower shop called Fairytale Flowers.

Cute name, I thought, thinking of *Sprookje*.

That night at dinner with my friend Coco in San Clemente, my heart kicked me... hard. It had another idea, as with seventeen years prior to go on the search. This time the idea came through another—literal—sign...Fairytale Flowers. My head resisted.

"Send Him flowers!" my heart said.

"Send Him flowers? What are you talking about...send Him flowers? Have you lost your, oh, wait, that's me, and I'm right here. No!" my head said.

"Send Him flowers! You know where!"

"What? Because a sign said Dutchman across from a medical facility, and magically I know where?"

"Yes! Send Him flowers! King's Day is coming up. It will be nice to do it then."

"No! No, no, no!" My head told my heart. "Absolutely not! Stop telling me that. I'm not sending Him flowers. Who do we even send them to? We don't have a name! For twenty years we haven't had a name. No, I'm not sending flowers."

Ohhhh, but what the heart wants to do, does not let up on.

Alllllll the way back across the country from Los Angeles to New York City, my heart would *not* give up. It pestered *relentlessly* to send Him flowers, on an absolute guess as to where. It was like Patrick Swayze keeping Whoopi awake in *Ghost* as she tries to block his singing out with pillows on her ears, until she *can't* take it anymore and agrees to help him. Great scene Whoopi...so funny! That was my heart to my head singing "*send Him flowers*," for three thousand miles.

The next day, like Whoopi, I gave in.

"All right! All right! All right! I'll send flowers wherever you want Mr. Heart. Just stop asking! But I'm doing it anonymously! We're not even sure if it's the right facility."

My heart figured if He didn't work there, the flowers and the energy of *twenty years* of gratitude would be paid forward, to *someone*, finally! Yes my heart was ready to erupt into the sky four stories high, to say THANK YOU. Yes, that would give the dying regret more peace.

Even if I guessed wrong, *somebody* would benefit from the intention, and have their day brightened with flowers. Whomever they were meant to find...they'd find; a Dutch Doctor, a sick patient's bedside, or some other essential worker who needed an unexpected uplift to their day. Yes! That sounded good, and felt good. Then I could let go as the fairy tale flower-power of good vibes spread to *someone*.

First, I went to Trader Joe's and bought myself some flowers, tulips. Yes, why not? I deserve flowers too! The next morning, with the nerves of 24-me surging, I went to Chelsea Florist with an anonymous note that said, 'For King-like kindness', and, after twenty years, I sent twenty tulips to possibly...*Him*. Addressed to 'The Dutch Doctor,' off they went, with no way of knowing whether my *complete* guess was right or not, and if, by the afternoon, He and I would make contact via flowers and a note...after twenty years.

The next day, I was walking in the West Village and saw one of the graffiti angel posts on a lamppost. A heart with the words inside, "Flowers remind us why rainy days are necessary." I don't know. Something inside me started bubbling, started going off, like electricity. A feeling budding that I may have guessed...right? That He actually worked there and received the flowers. How could that be? Another miracle? More magic?

I felt more peaceful. Even if the tulips didn't make it to Him, somebody was enjoying them. Perhaps that was what I was feeling...*someone's* vibration raised in happiness, with tulip beauty added to their day. It was also that day I saw the post for the first time: "The only magic I still believe in is love." And somehow, I can't logically explain the feeling, but it felt stronger, that after *twenty* years we had made positive contact again.

Throughout the week, I felt so serene inside, so...light. The pressure that had built inside, about hurting an old friend—twice—began releasing throughout my mental, emotional, and energetic fields. Yes, I was aware that it was currently a one-sided friendship, and one through dreams. Yet no less special of a friendship, at least to one of the parties involved. Finally, an olive branch had been delivered... if I guessed correctly. But I was feeling more positive that it had. The stunning bliss that finally...He, Amsterdam Angel—possibly—*knew*, had me walking...no *skipping* on air all week. My heart was singing along with Celine and Peabo.

> *Tale as old as time*
> *True as it can be*
> *Barely even friends*
> *Then somebody bends*
> *Unexpectedly*
> *Just a little change*
> *Small to say the least*
> *Both a little scared*
> *Neither one prepared*
> *Beauty and the Beast.*

The Beast that I felt like nine months ago on my street that day finally had the chance...to bend.

***

Friday night, I had dinner plans with Liza in Tribeca. I'm not that familiar with Tribeca and was a bit turned around when I came up from the subway as to which way I needed to go. I ran into a guy who asked *me* for directions to the same restaurant. We were both lost, walking together, talking along the way. He asked me if I'd been to Pier 26 yet. He mentioned it had just been renovated and commented how nice of a job the city did on it. I told him I hadn't but would check it out sometime.

We arrived; I was shown to a table. Liza was running late. When she arrived she swooped around the corner with a bouquet of tulips presented in my face. She was feeling the excitement and rebirth of spring and wanted to share it. The energy felt full circle. The tulips I had sent out to Him days before returned through Liza as more tulips to me. I gasped a bit, my breath taken away. More confirmation? Had *He* really received them? Did I *really* guess right?

Saturday afternoon the sun was warm and shining, a beautiful spring day to read in the grass at Christopher St. Pier. After about an hour, I remembered the man from the night before and decided to walk downtown to Pier 26 and explore. By the time I arrived, I had worked up a sweat and was a bit tired. One of the first benches I came to, I sat down. It faced north. After taking a sip of water and setting the bottle down, I sat back and looked up. There, staring at me from the old warehouse on pier 40, was an enormous sign, in all caps, *gigantic* letters bursting their grand capitalized message: I WANT TO THANK YOU!

I can't make anyone feel what I felt in that moment. It pales to try and put it in words. Perhaps, like the moment after a magician does his trick, and the audience is left pondering, *how* did *he do that?* I was submerged in pure wonderment. I felt both the biggest explosion of joy bursting out of me like rays of light, and the most serene peace on the deepest level. Was this a kundalini rising?

My heart, my soul, my gut...*knew*—with no *logical* explanation to the feeling, no "proof"—in that moment—that my guess was *right*. The Dutch Doctor *was* Amsterdam Angel, and I'd made contact. I couldn't believe it. I just couldn't believe it. After twenty years, there was positive contact.

Even though my ego would try to get its unsolicited opinion heard, to leave room for a *slight* margin of error, and be realistic that, until *He* confirmed it, there was still the *slightest* chance I was wrong. Still, beneath the surface of that lingering doubt, the feeling deeper within, pulsating *stronger*, was that the tulips reached Him. I couldn't prove it. I just felt it to be true in every cell of my being. I felt such a release, a twenty-year release, a dying regret from the last life beginning to shift.

It was as if the man from the night before had been put in his path, like in the film *The Truman Show,* to make me aware of Pier 26, to lead me to the message of thanks. Perhaps, His own sentiment was expressed from His thoughts, sending out a vibration, a telepathic message that guided me to this four stories high message of gratitude?

Energy.

I don't know. We'd have to ask Him.

Oh, fuck! Why didn't I sign the card? I then thought.

I didn't know that I was going to be right! That I would guess right! That's why!

I wonder if He will figure out it was I? Ohhhhh, why would He? He's ice dagger mad at me. Why would He think someone that avoids Him twice would be sending Him flowers? Ohhhhh, whhhhyyyy didn't I sign it?

I carried on to the East Village. The graffiti angels seemed prevalent that day. Creating messages when all strung together: "It's All Happening" on one shirt in a store window; "Love Always Wins" on another girl walking by; "Love" in chalk on the sidewalk before me labeling my path...the path of love.

***

The following mid-afternoon, I returned to the Christopher Street Pier. I wanted it to become a relaxing place for me. Where I could read. Sit in the grass. Look at the Hudson and have peace there again. There was still a tinge of melancholy with *the* area, just south of the pier where my tower moment occurred eight months prior. The rawness of the vibration of those minutes—screaming, crying, and sobbing—still rippled from that spot, and was tender to absorb when I was near it. I wanted that healed. So I began gravitating toward the pier, to layer peaceful moments and time in the area, to soothe and balance the pain of memories past.

I was sitting in the grass leaning against one of the curved benches on the right, reading my book and highlighting the resonating parts. There were other people around enjoying the sun as well. Sometimes it's too crowded, with music and louder talking than I care to hear. Although sometimes it is good music and I'm in the mood. On this particular day, there was a pleasant balance of both people and music; it was peaceful, Goldilocks just right. Felt *good* to have my feet in the grass with an interesting book, be near the water, with the sun shining, and spring blooming, a lovely way to spend a Sunday afternoon, the 2nd of May... to be exact.

I went to shift positions and looked up. As I lifted my head, my eyes landed in direct contact with an eye, glancing my way, for a *split* second. Before the eye turned away and the man it was attached to continued walking down the pier on the opposite side.

What? Is that Him?

Do a second look, do a second look! My mind pleaded to Him.

The man had blond-hair, gray T-shirt, gray shorts with a red stripe, black shoes with white trim. It *was* the same man as the one at my doorstep—even all bundled up—I could tell. Both those sightings, He looked like He had put on muscle, from His swimmer's build of the summer sighting. Had He been working out? Regardless, I was certain that all three sightings were indeed the same man. But was it really *Him*—Amsterdam Angel—Him? His eye turned away so quickly when I saw it.

Why? Didn't He want me to see Him? To talk to Him? Didn't He want to talk to me?

It made me nervous. Remembering the sighting at my doorstep, closed off energy, ice daggers. I didn't want to hurt Him again. My god, He was the *last* person on the planet I'd want to hurt.

Flashbacks to the searches in Amsterdam were triggered all over again: the insecurities, the sadness, the foolish feeling, going up to take a second look. Again, relying on that second look of interest from *Him*; that never happened all those times...*this* time. I remained sitting in the grass wondering as I watched someone who I believed was Him walking down the pier.

Ahhhh, why didn't He come up to me? He had to have walked right behind me, if He had walked to the end of the pier and turned to circle-back down the other side where I saw Him. Why didn't He say Hi? Was He still mad or hurt by my walk-bys?

Further down the pier He ran His hand through His blond hair, almost in a nervous way. Why? Then the glimpse of eye I caught before it turned replayed in my mind. It looked nervous, felt nervous.

Why, why would He be nervous? Fuck! I didn't sign the card? Fuck! Why didn't I at least put an 'M' on the friggin' card? Ughhh. He probably didn't think I was approachable. Probably wasn't sure it was me who sent the tulips, and even if He did think it was I, figured if I wanted to interact with Him...I would have signed the frickin card! Ahhhh, why didn't I do it this way, or that way!

Beautiful Man from the Dark! I didn't know I would guess right! I didn't think that you wanted to interact with me! I know it probably didn't feel great to be walked past! I thought that You wanted nothing to do with me!

I didn't sign the card because...I don't know! I was scared that it was a wrong guess; that I'd look like a fool for addressing flowers to 'The Dutch Doctor,' if I guessed wrong. I just wanted to put some beauty into His life, like He had done for me for years, in support and inspiration through dream.

Why did I have to do it anonymously?

Once the shock penetrated that this was *the* potential reality...my reality: that the months and months of wondering, since Amp first mentioned Him, if the impossible of decades was possible—that the Dutch Doctor is Amsterdam Angel—it took *that* long to absorb as my reality. But now it seemed it was. And I had let Him walk by...again? Fuck we were like two teenagers. I don't want any more ice daggers. He doesn't want to be unacknowledged...again. Ahhh, why can't I jump out of this loop?

I'm frozen. Trying to talk to a boy—*the* boy—*the first* love. My heart had been frozen in time for Him. By *sprookje* poison—the Catholic Church Curse, not allowing my heart to beat for a boy, to be given to a boy, to love a boy. The curse that prevented me from talking to Him the *first* time still cursed me! With the regret of each sighting, the longing to meet again for twenty years, now piled on top. The deeper I went the tenderer it was getting. Clueless as to why I couldn't talk to *the* boy—now a man—who potentially just walked by, to see if it was *Him*.

When I *would* go up to a blond-hair blue-eyed man, it was wrong.

Ohhhhh, Beautiful Man from the Dark if You only knew. The disappointment that followed when it wasn't You, time after time, wore on my heart. The times when I cowered, when I felt it could have been You...torturing. My heart would plummet to my feet. Why when I give You up...do You appear?

Now Christopher Street Pier became a bittersweet spot after that day. I couldn't believe it. The joy at seeing Him again, now I am sure, it *is* Him. Mixed with the regret of another failure to launch. My *god*, what was wrong with me?

How could the setting have been any better, a perfect reunion spot, from the darkroom of Cockring to the sunlight at Christopher Street Pier? Fuck, I couldn't make this stuff up. I don't know if I'm that creative. Rather, I'm simply reporting the events that occurred. The events that if I didn't live them, didn't write them down, see them in black and white, *I* wouldn't believe them.

The synchronicities felt so movie-like that week. This *only* happens in the movies! Yet it *was* happening. As the shirt in the shop window, the day before foreshadowed, "It's *All* Happening." Didn't I believe in my own movie's messages that were being sent?

Doctor! Doctor! Give me the news! I got a bad case of loving my muse.... Which is You. I think...I'm pretty sure.

Ahhhh, magical whiplash!

The impossible accomplished? I was absolutely dumbfounded.

For the next couple weeks, I did go back to the pier on Sundays around the same time. Maybe it was His routine to jog the river every Sunday...but no sign. *Fuck, now He would probably avoid the pier like the plague on Sundays. I fucked it up...*again!

***

A few weeks later, He made a brief appearance in a dream. I was in a coffee shop, and He popped up like a jack-in-the-box from behind the counter, smiling a catch-me-if-you-can smile. Ahhhhh, if only I could! But I couldn't! Not in my dreams. Not in the third dimension, always unexpected with His appearances. Who are you elusive Dutch unicorn doctor?

The deeper I dig, the more I try to comprehend this connection, the more a bottomless abyss of understanding it keeps becoming. *Why?* Why *You*? Why do *You* come to me like this?

Why did He, out of billions of people, come to me all these years as a friend in dreams during poignant moments? Psychology driven people will have one opinion, New Age folks another. Believe me, I've heard and been open to them both. And why did He appear in the third dimension after I had been thinking of or writing about Him?

No one can *actually* prove one way or another why this has occurred, including me. All I could do was relay the events, including everything I mentioned herein about the directions and experiences of my life and the dreams of the person who has "come along" at pivotal moments, and how these dreams inspired me in the ways that they did. These are the facts...of *my* life.

As summer approached, I couldn't kick the regret of how the latest sighting played out weeks before. I thought back to *The Alchemist,* a book I lived by, quite literally, when I first began the search. I was like Santiago, the protagonist, going on a journey for love all of those years ago in Amsterdam.

After that first week on the original search, feeling blue and lonely, I walked the streets near Leidseplein looking for a restaurant. I circled back to the first one I passed, a Brazilian steakhouse with a beautiful young woman out front barking for business. I felt alone. Her energy felt more welcoming and genuine than the other restaurants vying for my business.

"You gave me the warmest and only smile out of all the other restaurants I saw," I said to her. "So I came back to you."

"Thank you. *Always* go with the first; it's usually the best," she replied with a wink and another smile while showing me to a table outside. "Let me grab you a menu and some water."

I wish I had; I thought about Him as her comment about going with the first—love, in this case—replayed in my mind while she was away. When she returned, she snapped me back into the moment.

"Why do you look so sad?" she asked, picking up on my distant, non-present energy.

She felt sisterly, and I felt comfortable openning up to her. I wanted to talk about Him to *someone*, to make Him real, keep Him alive. I was beginning to feel it was all just a dream.

"I met a boy here three years ago. I didn't ask His name. I came back hoping to find Him. But I haven't."

"Ahhhh, you are in love with Him?"

"Yes. But I feel foolish because I don't know *anything* about Him. I was too shy and ran away. It felt so wonderful to just *be* with Him."

"And you came back...just because of that? How you felt with Him?"

"Yes," I said. "That feeling was all that I needed."

"I understand. But you have love. *All* around you, in you, *right* in front of you. Just look at me. Here you are, sitting here, I have just met you, and *I* love you."

She picked up on my confused look at her statement and continued.

"You tell me you have crossed an ocean because you took a chance at finding a boy that you don't know *anything* about, not even His name, because you liked how you *felt* with Him. I love *you* for *that*. I don't need to know anything more about you, not even *your* name."

She uplifted me when I needed it to continue on like Santiago. Now, seventeen years later, it seemed I had been sidelined in my own story to the supporting character in *The Alchemist* of the crystal merchant every time there was a sighting. The merchant never took a chance on his dream to go to Mecca.

Send more flowers. Write a note this time! My heart encouraged.

Yes, that is what I would do. I became absolute in my conviction: I would *not* be the merchant in my own story. I would *not* let the Dutch Mecca remain an oasis.

I am Santiago! Not the merchant!

But my ego kept poking in with his opinion. It still doubted that it could truly be Him. It cautioned me against writing the letter. Even for all of my belief in magical proof, my intuition, and my dreams, my ego wanted to stay safe. Stay safe from hoping *any* longer. Stay safe from believing that *the* dream of dreams could come true and was *really* in my neighborhood.

Ahhhhh, Celine! You sang such truth!

I'm scared, so afraid to show I care...

Stay safe from the potential reality—after all *this*—that, take it away, Ms. Dion...

> *Ooohhh, what*
> *If there's another one*
> *He's thinking of*
> *Maybe He's in love*
> *I'd feel like a fool.*

Yes, Celine! I can absolutely relate to The Fool feeling.

But most of all, my ego wanted to stay safe from waking up from *the* dream into the potential reality—or the potential nightmare—and my biggest fear to both me's of a *twenty-year-long* unrequited notion. My ego knew full well that after *all* this, there might not be a response to the letter...at all. Yes, perhaps best to keep dreaming—like the crystal merchant—and writing. Besides, it may not even reach Him. It may not even be...Him.

But I *believe it is Him!* My heart spoke up and overruled my head. *We are Santiago! And if it is Him—regardless of a response—then, He must know.*

With the anniversary of my overdose approaching, the pressure built. I knew what it was like to have a dying regret. In those first minutes of realizing I was not dead, as I flashed back to meeting Him in Amsterdam, the regret I felt was for not meeting Him again, that He didn't get to know how I felt about Him, about our time together, and what it produced.

Feeling a dying regret when you realize you're not dead as it rushes to the surface, yes, there is sadness, of course. Having the regreted walk down the street on a sunny day weeks into the second life, is nothing less than a miracle. If it *really* is Him, the chance to rectify *the* impossible regret of my life, was *here*...and *now*.

I *had* to send a letter.

My *Boys in the Band* phone call in the form of a play (although a *wildly* creative idea) would take much longer to get out into the world...and to Him. I've learned with Joe, Mohammad, and Mike, there are no guarantees. Plus, with the impact of my own near death, the simple reality that it could come for me—again—or for Him at any moment led to a resolution. I had to make a switch: a *Boys in the Band* phone call in the form of...a letter.

Remaining optimistic, He just might like to receive such a letter and just *might* respond. Ahhh but what to write? What to write?

I was a mix of opinions. The teenager in me—who was inside 24-me—still frozen in the context of Him, as a first love—was mixed inside a 45-year-old.

45-me was more logically driven. Aware that our experience together was only romantic and erotic, he wanted the tone of the letter to be sans expectations of us picking up where we left off; and that I was capable of a platonic cup of coffee in a room with light...and would know how to talk to Him this time. Or share in being the co-creators of the play as it moved forward to production, for a unique life experience for us both. 45-me also wanted to respect whatever was going on in His life—struggles, stress, romance, all of it—and knew a friendly approach was best.

But 24-me wanted his two cents used as well; the hope for romance still flickering. He wanted Him to know it *was* special, that it *did* mean something to me. More than He could know; three books, a play, a song.

Both me's wanted to share the excitement of the play. How everything felt as if it came full circle, from being right on the verge of quitting, not completing the series, to cutting it short. Then, the inspiration to create something that helped me heal, that I believed in, and thought could help other people. Express the joy to share it with Him, as a friend, or a creative partner. Who better to share it with than The Muse who had made my writing come to life?

The different aged versions of me wanted to apologize; a nearly twenty-year sorry that had been building since the connection was recognized back in the pink house. Plus, I wanted to add a second sorry for walking by a second time on my street *that* day. And without going into too much detail, I wanted to tell Him how dark it had been in my life both times His bright light came shining in.

But the teenager inside was driven by both the possibility and fear that it had been our only shot to make contact. And I was afraid he would neither forgive the walk by's or false name given, especially as I had yet to forgive myself.

Lastly, the three parts of me dreamed of meeting Him again. Jeeeezzz, no pressure there to fulfill somebody's dream! Energetically, it was a convoluted ball of yarn.

Regardless, one weekend while visiting Liza in The Hamptons I sat at a picnic table by the bay in Sag Harbor—ironically—near the windmill, and composed what felt like the most important letter of my life. Nearly a year into the unexpected turn of events of the previous one, the dying regret was addressed, and finally, He would know. Yes, that would give me more lasting peace, moving forward, regardless of whether He responded or not. I regained enough love for *myself* to want that peace for me, and if there were any hurt feelings, perhaps some peace for Him.

The following week, one late spring afternoon in June, the letter along with white orchids was sent to Him. Then my head told my heart to let go. Again. Knowing *He* would *know*, I could do so with more peace in my second life. So I hoped.

***

Did I think He would call right away? 24-me hoped so, of course. That first weekend was the most nerve-wracking, wildly wondering what He thought about such a gesture. The stranger in the night, from so long ago who couldn't say "hi" now had four pages of words to say; that was just the letter, wait until He found out there were *books*.

I met my Swedish friend Mila in the park for a picnic, to help calm my nerves and insecurities. I read her the letter to make sure that it was okay—what I wrote, that I sent it, and along with more flowers.

"Darling, we're European, we've love that shit. It's in our genes. It's a beautiful letter," she point-blank reassured me.

But the foolish feeling returned from the initial search. I felt stupid for sending the letter. I should have said this or not said that. I felt silly for calling Him a hero to me, placing Him on a pedestal—like He put me on a pedestal by squatting before me. Even though it was—is—so romantic to me. Until *afterward*, understanding about energy, how those actions make for an unbalanced connection, making one greater than the other...instead of equal. All of the thoughts rushing through my head had the effect of both my finger and toenails being chomped right off... waiting...hoping He would call *that*—first—weekend.

Yet the adult in me realized it may be a complete 180 to receive a letter from the stranger who couldn't say 'hi'...until now, confessing he'd always hoped we would meet again. I'm sure it was a lot to absorb. If the situation were reversed, how would I feel? I'd be intrigued for sure and curious to find out more. Still, I didn't know how it felt to be in His wooden shoes or what was going on in His head and heart each time our paths crossed. I was grounded in that.

***

Not long after the letter was sent, He started to come back into my dreams more frequently. A week later I dreamt I was being flown in a plane. I was in the co-pilot's seat and was not aware of who the pilot was. This person was showing me how to fly a plane before landing us to take a break. Afterward, before I stepped inside the plane, I saw two men standing outside. One was Him, and He looked a bit melancholy. The other person was the man I was with when I had my near-death experience. I stepped into the flight deck and sat in the pilot's seat. I began getting situated for takeoff. After a few moments, I turned toward the co-pilot's seat to see it empty. I wondered if anyone was coming with me. I turned to look down the fuselage to see if someone was going to board. I waited and wondered for a moment before waking up.

It had only been a week since sending the letter. I still felt insecure. I tried to interpret the dream: I hoped to meet Him, but there was nothing left I could do. For this to be accomplished, it involved His desire and free will, or the gods finagling another run-in—that I wouldn't fuck up. Neither appeared to be happening.

Maybe a break from New York was needed. It had been an intense year with so much healing. Perhaps that was the purpose of this; to help me to examine my life of the previous twenty years via a conversation with Him, as the reflection of myself, to really *heal*, to really dig *deep,* and do all the shadow work to uncover and heal any remaining buried wounds. Now, He knew, and there was peace spreading, anchoring in, where the regret had lain buried.

The following day was the vision I had after yoga class, in savasana posture, where my image appeared instead of His. Celine and Barbara's words resonated truth in my reality. Love did feel like the gift I gave myself in sending the letter. Perhaps Mr. Aciman's book *Find Me* was not foreshadowing a message from *Him*. But rather it was a message from future-me, to the *"me"* that was lost and being transformed over the previous fifteen months since Mike's death, and my near death.

Find—the new—Me.

And to do that, the final step to finding my first love—where *Sprookje* birthed its ending—was sending the letter. Everything I wrote to Him, I wrote to myself. It was all there, the adoration and desire, the regret and sorrow too. He knew I believed in magic and miracles. Although He could not fathom how much so without the backstory, just Him walking down my street that day was all the proof I needed to believe.

Well, now nearly a year later, it was out of my hands. With no response toward the end of the month, 45-me accepted, yes, love Him and let Him go. Run to something...to Amsterdam. In honoring myself, my life, and other dreams, it felt time to explore the Amsterdam dream that had been put on hold a year prior; to rise again, cross paths with Him, be inspired to write again, and heal more deeply, in ways I never could have imagined. While 24-me felt the restless itch to run away, felt his frozen heart from the *sprookje* curse crack—like the first crack of ice when one more step further onto the frozen pond is taken—at the possibility we would never meet again.

Yes, it felt like the right time to go to Amsterdam. He knew. He had my number. And for a few weeks, chose not to use it. I could travel. Art was moving from the flat by Oosterpark that I had known intimately for over a decade, where the majority of my writing was done. I wanted to spend a month in the old 'hood, say goodbye, and help Art move into the new home. So I began to make arrangements to go to Amsterdam for a couple of months, and to let Him go.

Yet in the weeks before I did, He began traveling back to me more frequently in dreams. At the beginning of the month, I had a dream where I saw Him sitting at Lollino's new location—which there wasn't one as far as I knew in the 3D world— somewhere in the city. He was smiling His big smile, the playful yet ever-frustrating catch-me-if-you-can smile. "I" was not there yet. When I made my "entrance" in the dream at the cafe, Amp excitedly told me He was *just* there.

"Where did He go?" I asked both with happiness and anxiety.

"I don't know," Amp replied. "But I think He mentioned He was moving."

"Where?"

"I don't know, I think the Upper West Side? I don't remember, I'm sorry."

I went to the bathroom and began chain-smoking at the urinal. Lollino came in shortly afterward pleading with me that I must stop smoking...it wasn't good for me. And that was it.

Again it was a bittersweet experience, sweet to see Him, bitter only in dream. It brought up another anxiety from deep within that began around the start of that year. An anxiety that, in order to let go, and heal...I *had* to find Him...as *soon* as *possible*. What if He was on a year work visa and leaving America, or He had moved to another neighborhood, or borough, or job? Had the East Village served its purpose? Was it just for me to date myself? Take me out of my comfort zone in order to reintegrate with life again? Was I wasting my time going there? The anxiety of being so close to a dream, only to have it slip away...flooded me. It was a shock to my heart like Phil watching Nemo be swept away into the vast ocean, leaving Phil completely bewildered as to how *Finding Nemo* would even be possible.

I was Dumbo frantically falling through the sky from that fear as the white feather dream of Him begins slipping away. I grasp tighter and tighter to it in order to fly. Yes, I was plain old—*Dumb*-o, my inner teenager beating myself up for a stupid old dream, that seemed to dissolve away more and more with each passing day.

Eleven days later, another dream occurred. He was a contestant on a game show. He was smiling. His eyes were shining, happy, and excited to be playing. I was trying to get a closer look, crouching around the podium to see if it was *really* Him, while trying not to disturb the game. He was winning, hence the big smile. The audience was cheering. Of all the prizes, the one I was hoping He would choose...was me. I had big orange orchids and smaller white ones waiting to give to Him.

Not long after that dream, I had another one. He appeared with Bas, another blue-eyed, blond Dutch man that I had met in Amsterdam three years before. I saw Bas on Grinder and his picture stunned me at first because he looked so much like Him. My heart started beating faster wondering, if, after all these years I would find Him on Grinder?

Bas and I met and hearts floated for me. A couple of months later, I made a gesture that hinted at romantic interest. I was hesitant if it was "too soon" to make a move like *that* after one meeting and some texts back and forth. Whatever that means with some conditioned societal "rules" on dating, that don't *really* exist...if you just be yourself.

But I took His lead from the darkroom as inspiration. I always respected it as courageous and thought of it as so sexy—still—all these years later. If you feel something, *say it!* He felt something and expressed it. So with that reference, I did the same with Bas.

Silence.

There wasn't even the *sound* of crickets it was so silent.

No response.

I must have had the insecurity of the 3D experience with Bas in my subconscious. Now playing out 2½ years later through a dream concerning the letter and orchids I sent to Him. The insecurity, combined with the fear that it would turn out the same way with Him...with silence. In the dream, He was looking to Bas for advice. Being the newest blond hair blue-eyed Dutch man that this person...me...was making a move toward. He was asking Bas for advice.

"What do I do about it," He said to Bas with a bit of anxiety.

"Oh don't worry. You don't have to do anything if you don't want. He won't send any more letters," Bas assured Him.

The next dream was in a hospital setting. There was an entity of energy in the shape of a human that was quickly dashing out of the hospital, not wanting to be seen. Perhaps a boyfriend of His who was leaving, out of the picture of His life, because then He and I were in a car on a road. I was driving Him to work like a boyfriend would.

When we entered the hospital parking lot, the dream—as dreams sometimes do—became strange. The cars were hung like beef in a cooler and cost $2.50 per day to park...or rather hang. I gave Him $10. He insisted that I didn't need to do that. I insisted that He let me buy him four days' worth of hanging his car. He smiled sweetly and accepted.

The interpretation I guessed was that perhaps He had been dating someone, and now I had a shot with Him. But still no phone call in the 3D, so perhaps an incorrect interpretation or wishful hoping from my subconscious. It seemed as if all insecurities around Him were coming from my subconscious and being reflected in dream through Him to feel and heal via self-love.

He was not the only muse to visit me in dream. My other one did as well, Gloria. Like a girl—muse—friend showing up to comfort me during boy—muse—friend troubles...waiting, hoping for Him to call. Oh, it was soooo nice to see Gloria! She had not visited me in dream in *many* years. We were hanging out on the second floor of a beautiful mansion, cozy on a couch in front of an enormous window overlooking a sprawling estate. She was sharing a bit about herself and what it is like to be her.

"It's really a *lot* of fun," she said afterward.

I chuckled to myself at how adorable she was, the way she said it.

I'll bet it is Gloria. I'll bet it is, I thought.

I woke feeling happier, both to see Gloria and from the consoling effects of a girlfriend helping to shoo away the blues about a boy.

The last dream I had of Him, before I left for Amsterdam was a scene of Art hosting a dinner party in Amsterdam. I had "arrived" there and was—apparently—living my "new" life. I'd accepted that I went after one dream that didn't quite pan out how I hoped, and was now going after another. I was helping Art clear the table to work in the kitchen. Then in an instant, His *energy* swooshed in with a message, "Don't forget about me."

Ahhhh, hello, Beautiful Man from the Dark. I haven't forgotten about you in twenty years. Believe me I've tried. What makes you think I'll be successful at it now, or ever in this incarnation?

The strange and new experience was that the message was audible. It was as if I actually heard the words, "Don't forget about me." As soon as they were said, I felt Him energetically and immediately woke up. Stunned, I second-guessed if I had actually *heard* what my gut felt it had. Days later, I was off to Amsterdam to try and move forward.

***

In Amsterdam, I switched gears. I checked in with Art and where he was at with the business, what was potentially needed, and when on my end. The pandemic changed and slowed down the progress of creating it. I vowed not to do anything with the play.

I told my therapist before I left that I didn't think I could put out the piece. Not after the letter, with still no response. How could I make Him my professional life, thinking of Him by writing about Him, with the current reality of no response? It seemed sadomasochistic to my heart. I didn't feel I could separate the two without it being painful. Perhaps all of the writing was just for personal healing and not meant to be shared. Maybe I should give up as I had a year ago.

My therapist disagreed about the writing. She thought I could separate the professional aspect from the individual. And she wanted more, more about Mike, and more about my PTSD.

More! I thought of the dreaded notion as my eyebrows rocketed up. I knew there was more to add about the start of the drug use, the suicidal thoughts, and the still tender regret about Mike.

But, noooooo!

No more!

I can't!

It hurts!

I had never written about such painful experiences so soon after them. All the others were years later. No. Absolutely not! I wasn't ready, and maybe I never would be. The fear of sharing such intimate details was getting to me too. My family, my friends—even though I knew most would understand, I did have hesitation because of my friend Mila.

It was the previous winter. We were heading to a coffee shop in the village. I decided to open up to her about the overdose, feeling safer person by person. There was more distance from it for me. I was more comfortable talking about it. But when I told her causally as we both walked down Bleecker St. near Bookmarc, Mila stopped dead on the street, took a wide step, bent over, put her head between her legs, and started hyperventilating. I laughed nervously not knowing what was happening or how to help. I thought she was going to vomit. It took a moment to sink in that it was the words I had said that created it. I felt horrible. It was the first visual reaction of someone I loved absorbing the words I'd spoken.

"Darling, I'm *so* sorry," I said. "I didn't know the thought of my death would have an impact like that. I'm so sorry. I am healing."

Afterward, she told me that she felt something was wrong the previous summer. My Whitney-like physical appearance was apparent to her that something was happening, and she wondered. Perhaps it was naïve of me to think I was hiding it from everyone. Good friends always sense when something's happening…that's why they're good friends.

So to go deeper, write, and reveal more of the story when it could have an impact like that on someone I loved? No, no more of that. It had already become much longer than a one-person show should be and more like a lyrical poem with stage directions.

Each time I added more, delved deeper, it was like learning to walk and move forward through life again. But instead of my legs being paralyzed, it was my heart. Each painful step, clutching the parallel bars, falling, wanting to give up, to crawl to my heart's wheelchair.

Don't ask for more!

Even though I knew deep down that my therapist was right, adding more only meant more healing for me.

***

Amsterdam was my time to fall down from the parallel bars and crawl to a potential new life. But my therapist's words kept echoing from across the pond. I did my best to avoid them. Unless opportunities came to me—without seeking them out—I was committed to not doing anything with the play.

The only two that did were Doris, a filmmaker friend who asked what I'd been working on, and Martijn, a friend in the theatre world who inquired as well. I told Martijn I decided to give up writing. Then life foiled that plan. I was knocked over with inspiration. Rather, the muse shocked the hell out of me with a three-dimensional appearance...and I began writing again.

He laughed, and asked to see it. I hesitated for weeks. But eventually, I sent it to them both. The rest of the time, I spent disconnecting from America. I enjoyed the old flat, and moved into the new house. There was only one problem.

I couldn't escape reminders of Him everywhere! His energy, like a Siamese twin, came along, reminding me, as the dream, "Don't forget about me." He first popped in mediation upon my arrival. After being replaced with my own image in June, helping me to feel I'd come full circle back to self-love, appreciating His reflecting role in that...now He was back.

Multiple times throughout the day, *everyday, everywhere* I went I would see the word Angel, or *Engel*—the Dutch version of it—on people's shirts or in shop windows...or variations of it, Los **Angel**es. Or I'd hear the word from someone's mouth describing someone they knew or in songs.

Every—*frigging*—where!

And it's not even His name!

Ahhhhh—why? Why did I have to pick Angel? Why Amsterdam Angel? Why couldn't I have chosen Harold? Yes, Amsterdam Harold. How many Harolds would I have seen? None! Ugghhhhh, come on universe! I'm trying to love and let go. Again! For, like, the one thousandth one hundred and eleventh time!

And white orchids? Everywhere! White orchids were in both shop and home windows. Seared into my mind.

Jeeezzz! Why does everybody have white orchids everywhere? What's wrong with a little color people? Why did I pick white orchids to give to him? Are you kidding me? It's the Netherlands for fucks sake! Where were the tulips? Come to think of it, that wouldn't have helped either. Do I have to go to Antarctica to keep myself from any reminders of Him? With my luck, the penguins would probably be making snow angels. Ahhhh, Eternal Sunshine of the Spotless Mind...*please strike me!*

***

Then one day, I was sitting at Stroom's café window in De Pijp after a yoga class having a coffee and looking outside at the people passing by. There were a few picnic tables, and I noticed the backs of a young man and woman holding hands approach one and sit down. He straddled the bench to face her so I could see his face.

My heart skipped a beat. It was a striking resemblance to Him in our younger years. It was so sweet to watch their young love blooming. He was *really* into her. His body language spoke it all, leaning in, being affectionate. He didn't take his eyes off her and was smiling continuously. He sparkled just to be near her. She was one lucky woman.

Out of nowhere, it hit me, another crack in the ice of 24-me's heart. My eyes watered, and tears dropped. I thought of the missed opportunity for that to be us in Amsterdam, all those years ago. Yes, perhaps it wouldn't have lasted. I wasn't even living there. But perhaps...who knows. That was the problem. It was looking like I never would.

I cried because of the pain from the anger buried deep that was bubbling up at the Catholic Church for stealing my innocence. For ingraining in me that I was a bad person for my thoughts and desires. Imagine having a first date with the gender someone knew they wanted, a kiss at a bowling alley instead of a dark alley by a dumpster, an after school roller skating party, being picked by a boy you wanted to be picked by for the couples skate, or for prom. I get choked up typing this.

No, I don't need sympathy.

I used to laugh it off in my mind—my introduction into the gay world with the Red Light District and sex in parks. Yes, on the surface, I will admit, there was a rush and eroticism to the majority of those experiences, completely lost in the passion of the moment. Yet, it was also the only way I was able to do *it* in the first place.

But the mental and emotional anguish that came afterward was crippling and unnecessary. Certainly the stress of it strained my health and probably took time off my life. And on the other side of that same coin was the buried truth covered by laughter. The pain was— apparently—still there. So I let the tears drop. I didn't care who noticed each time I wiped away the tears for experiences I never got to have.

Experiences perhaps taken for granted by heterosexuals; none of this might not even cross their minds. And for even younger generations of LGBTQIA who are coming out in high school or before, who know *that* option exist...that you can love whom you were *born* to love. I still laugh with bittersweet disbelief each time I hear of people coming out younger and younger.

My godson came out at eleven...*fifteen years* before I did. While I'm *absolutely* thrilled and proud of him and the progress made in society in the last twenty years, it also leaves me, at times trying to comprehend how my life might have been had I come out at eleven or any of the other ages I hear of people coming out. Which, of course, I cannot fathom. My heart encourages my mind to let go of what-could-have-been scenarios and return to the present.

The younger generation may never know—though, many unfortunately in other parts of the country and world still do—all the pain and self-hatred those before them experienced, the internal war fought with their *selves* and the external fight for civil rights.

Just as I may take for granted what it was like for my grandfather or father, who both fought wars over seas for the freedoms I have enjoyed, perhaps the younger generations take for granted the mental, emotional, and physical freedoms paved by the sacrifices of generations before.

Regardless, these struggles gave them the foundation to love who they love more safely and peacefully. And that is a wonderful thing.

Not long after that day at Stroom, I was in a bookstore browsing when my eyes were drawn to the title of one book, followed by the first name of an author of another book right underneath it. It read like an encouraging message from the other side, from her...

I Couldn't Be More Proud...Gloria.

Occasionally, my wanders around the city would take me down Warmoesstraat and past the old Cockring. It turned into another gay club after Cockring closed—the Meat Rack. Then remained a gay club after that—I believe Club Fuxx—yet I think women were allowed in that version.

Currently, and for several years now, it's been called Stone's Café, a café in the afternoon and a club at night. I had not been in the space in many years. I checked out Meat Rack when it opened, but not since then.

From the outside it had changed a lot. The boarded up entrance, with only one small barred window, at the top half of the Dutch door entrance of Cockring—which created the mysterious allure of what was behind it—was now open with big windows that provided a look inside from the street and seating at the front. My curiosity was never enough to go inside—until, one day.

I walked in around 4:00 p.m. It looked like it was just opening. The young men half my age—probably pooping their diapers or not even born yet when He and I met—cleaning tables near the front windows warmly greeted me when I passed. I was the only customer in there.

I climbed the stairs near the entrance. The next level had changed a bit; it was more open. The bar was now against the wall. In the days of Cockring it was more toward the center, providing seating all around it. I approached the bar to see two twenty-something girls behind it—that was definitely a new experience. I'd never seen females in Cockring. They were friendly and welcoming to their first customer.

"Hi, what may I get for you?" one girl said.

"Do you have any coffee?" I said.

"Yes," she replied.

"I'll take a decaf, please."

She paused and looked at me like, well, like I was old.

"We don't have decaf."

Then she looked at her co-worker.

"How about a beer?" the co-worker said.

"No, I'll take a regular coffee then."

"Sure you don't want a beer?" she suggested again, perhaps thinking it was a better option if I didn't want caffeine. I thought it was cute.

"No, no, I'll do caffeine," I replied, while thinking, *I'll live on the edge.*

As she began preparing my coffee, I took a walk around. I was more curious, not about the main space, but about *what* had happened to the darkroom. I couldn't imagine there was one anymore. And there wasn't. Or, if there was, it was behind the enormous flat-screen playing videos; it covered the area where a door to one of the staircases to the darkroom was. The one I came out of, to see Him squatting before me.

There was still a staircase to the left, which led down to the middle landing where the bathroom was, as well as the entrance of a second, narrow winding stairwell that led up to the darkroom on the other side, while another staircase led to the dance floor. I continued walking down it to see what had changed.

The dance floor on the lower level was pretty much the same layout. The bar was moved slightly down toward where the stage for the strippers and sex shows was. It was more of a heterosexual environment, whatever that means anymore. I went back up to get my coffee and stopped on the middle landing. There was still a bathroom, but no entrance to the stairwell that went to the darkroom. It was as if the darkroom had been sealed in memoriam to another time.

I returned to the bar to pick up my coffee and walked to a stool and ledge at the wall—near *the* spot of the last kiss—to sit down. Still, no one else had arrived. I looked at the spot, and could still feel that moment, Him squatting there. Like Marilu's explanation of memory and those "firsts" that are seared in it. *That* moment was seared. The first time I saw His eyes in the light and He saw mine. I could feel the energy. I wasn't melancholy or sad...simply present in both moments simultaneously. The one nearly twenty-one years ago—like it never went anywhere—and the present one, mixed with the 'reality' of 'time' and its resulting differences: the space, the screen before me, the females behind me. It was all there, with me, along with Him...still.

***

Shortly before I returned to New York, He popped in for a visit to my meditation and then again in dream the following night. The vision was of His 5th dimensional self, smiling brightly at me with an affirming nod before turning to his other 5th dimensional spirit friends.

"*Hey* you guys! *Kom op!* (Come on!) I need your help! We have to get these two together on the other side, bump into each other—*something*. It's been twenty years!" He said to them.

"Twenty years!" was the surprised commotion of the others. "Yes that is *much* too long. Let's get to work!"

Oy vey, an ocean away and, *still,* He pops in, instilling hope in me with these visits, especially with the following night's dream. We were at my brother and sister-in-law's home, waiting for my other brother and his wife to go for a ride together; to get to know each other. It was the first time He met them. He and I were sitting on the couch affectionately close and cuddly, giggling in our own world.

But maybe the vision meant to get these two together in the dream world, or another dimension, or a parallel universe similar to how we ended the third book... and not *in the third dimension*, my mind tried to *logically* express his opinion, with the intent to help save my heart from reigniting hope, even though there's no telling the heart what to do, when the heart desires what the heart desires.

***

On my last night in Amsterdam I was walking on Reguliersdwarsstraat. It's the street the bar Havana was on. The place I first saw Him from my Juliet balcony. I was curious what Havana had become since it had closed many years before, not long before I arrived on the initial search in 2003. I wasn't even sure which building it was anymore. Businesses changed so much over the years. I looked up the address on my phone to make sure it was the right place and walked up to it. I laughed out loud..

Ahhhhh, the humor of the gods...perfection, I thought.

The serendipity couldn't have been more perfect with the current business in the former Havana spot: an American grill restaurant and café called...The Big Apple. As much as my ego wanted to stay safe, in *any* lingering doubt, that perhaps it wasn't *Him* whom I passed on my street *that* day, that He was *not* the new Dutch Doctor—standing in front of the building where I first saw Him, now nearly twenty-one years later—my intuition *screamed!*

Ja! (Yes!)

Het is Hem! (It is Him!)

In de Grote Appel! (In The Big Apple!)

I returned to The Big Apple as planned for the remainder of the year. I had *no* clue moving into 2022 what I would do. The pandemic had slowed the progression of Art's business, but I was still open to it. I didn't know if I wanted to do anything with the writing, reverting to the notion that perhaps it was just for my healing.

I relied on the adage, if you don't know what to do, don't do anything, and the answer will come. So I distracted myself. I re-decorated to shake the energy up. I took a Reiki workshop to learn more about energy and how to work with it. I concentrated on my health. I did everything I could to avoid thinking about Him.

Unfortunately, the more I tried to avoid it, the more I wondered if perhaps the dreams were premonitions. The last one I had felt too nice, having Him meeting my family. But perhaps it was just a dream. Like all of those years ago, rushing out of Cockring to Centraal Station to get back to Leiden and into my bed before the sun rose so the night would be just a dream. He—perhaps always would be—just a dream.

I tried to reconcile that I had *so* much to be thankful for in the last year. If nothing else, there were three *enormous* gratitudes that were more than enough to build a *strong* foundation for my new—second—life. I took a notecard and wrote them down:

I got a second chance at life.

I kept the promise to my mother.

And...

Hij weet. (He knows.)

Above those statements, I drew a peace sign and a heart next to it. Then enclosed them all in a triangle and placed it on my bulletin board. Moving forward, if I never got a chance to meet Him again, yes, those three sentiments were plenty to seed a happy life with; growing in a strong, *rock*-solid foundation of peace and love in my heart.

Never did I think that there would be *two* parts to the dream of Him: telling Him and meeting Him. I naturally assumed they would be accomplished at the same time. *Never* did I imagine—out of probably, I don't know, the hundreds of ways of where and how we would meet—that the opportunity presented to tell Him would be in the form of a letter...that He may not respond to.

Yet in the current moment that was the reality. And if it was to remain the reality, then the most important part had been accomplished. I could find peace with that.

***

I saw my therapist upon my return to America with the notion that the writing was for my healing. I would not proactively pursue it in the sense of putting it out in the world. I was open to her suggestion months earlier about giving more and going deeper—getting it *all* out—for *me*. After the first month of distracting myself with other activities...I began writing again.

I decided to include the start of the drug use and the suicidal thoughts. Plus, the—still—tender wound to write about, to feel, to *see* in black and white: the regret about Mike, not trusting in his unconditional love. I began getting it *all* out, going back to the parallel bars, for my heart to walk, to move onward again.

Every morning I was at the café early, traveling back to relive emotions that had never been processed. *Lodged* in my emotional body. Stuffed away for another day...or another lifetime.

As I dove inward, the muck at the bottom of the pond was stirred, rose to the surface, and released from my eyes. I couldn't believe how much I had cried since Mike. Over Mike and everything that happened since, to myself, and with Him. Essentially, I was astonished how so many tears could come out of one human body.

Yet, at the same time, I could absolutely believe it. I remembered thinking the same thing for Joe. Bewildered over the number of tears that flowed for three years after his death. Before finding acceptance in London, *excitedly* leaving for Amsterdam, afterward, to meet Mike, before I met...Him.

What a time-travel-like experience it is to return from revisiting those events and feelings, simply...profound. Like going back into a burning house...*my* house... my *home,* to save *myself.* Coughing out the smoke inhaled. Clearing the toxicity of shame from those thoughts, actions, and emotions once they were embraced with compassion, loved, and released, so I could return to the cleaner air of the present moment. Where I knew I was safe. When I knew I made it out of the fire safely. When I knew I'd—been—*saved* myself, as my home burned to the ground, giving me the chance to rebuild.

Emotional exhaustion was felt for much of the rest of the day. Triggering *myself* over and over with those moments of the past brought my mood down, made me grumpy, made me want to isolate so I wasn't moody with some innocent bystander.

But the deep inner knowing after twenty-five years of writing, feeling the pain in this way, reflecting, and getting it out, I understood would only make me stronger in mind and heart, and lighter in *being*. So I carried on each morning, while trying to operate in the three-dimensional present of November 2021. Trying to go with the flow, to get in touch with my heart, and observe the signs guiding me with what to *do* next with my life.

By the first weekend of November, as jarring and difficult as the week of going deeper within felt, I was nearly to the other side of getting all the emotions out. I was feeling better, lighter, knowing with each word on the page and out of me, the shame of my actions and thoughts toward myself were becoming more and more diluted with *radical* self-love and acceptance. The parts of myself the shame tried to reject, I loved and weaved back into the fabric of my life. While pursuing the writing—*actually* sharing the most recent version—was a thought that began to knock. Like Santiago in *The Alchemist,* I trusted an omen would come.

***

Friday night, I went to sleep and was awoken in the middle of the night around 1:30 a.m. He came to my mind. And, I don't know what to say. Whether it was intuition or 45-me breaking through, lovingly and paternally taking charge over 24-me—and his heart—by sending a message that permeated.

It was time.

Time to accept He may have chosen someone else romantically. Time to accept that the dream of ever meeting again—even for a "hello"—might *never* happen. Time to really face and feel *that* potential reality.

My head knew once the letter had been delivered, there was nothing left to do but let go. Hence, my head led my heart to Amsterdam to help distract it from the hope it still held on to for even a "hello." My head knew how these matters of the heart carry from lifetime to lifetime and tried to be compassionate and patient, knowing it was okay for my heart to take a little longer to catch up with my head's wisdom of letting go.

So at 1:30 a.m., 45-me woke 24-me up. I could have picked a better time, yet I suppose it was appropriate. The dream I was afraid of waking from had taken the chance by sending the letter. The rose's last petal was falling off, and it was time to walk down the dark, dusty road...we might never meet again. 45-me guided 24-me to the edge of the enchanted forest, which didn't seem so enchanted anymore; it was a much darker version of the forest from my ketamine session just months before.

Of course 24-me didn't want to go in! It was still too recent that he *had* been in a similar forest with Mike. Our younger selves carefree and playing for twenty-five years in that forest that suddenly turned dark, as the wind howled and blew, right before an entity from *A Quiet Place* snatched Mike away. Now I was back on the edge of that same forest, only it was *His* quiet—of no response—that seemed to snatch the dream away. And there is nothing scarier than a dream that feels as if it has died. Hell no! 24-me did not want to go back in and hesitated at the edge with 45-me.

"Look," 45 said to 24. "If you're choosing Him and He's potentially choosing someone else, who's choosing you? Nobody!"

"OK! OK! I get it! I get it! Nobody's choosing me." 24-me quickly responded while gripping—squeezing—on the remaining grains of sand of the dream.

"I'll choose me! I choose me! I do! I really do! It's okay if He doesn't want to be friends! It's okay if He loves someone else! I accept that! I already let go of both of those possibilities. I really have!"

"I know you have. But..."

"No! Don't say it! I know what you're going to say. You are me. I know what you're going to say. But don't say it! Please don't say it! I don't want to let go of that too! Please don't make me let go of that too!"

"It's time to accept you may never hear from Him, that you may never get to say hello...or learn His name."

"I told you not to say it!"

But with that thought spoken aloud—the frozen-in-time heart for Him received the final, irreversible crack in the ice—where you know if you don't run off the pond, you'll fall through.

So 24-me did.

Or rather, tried.

He tried to run away from that thought. Before he fell into the sobering cold reality that He/Amsterdam Angel/The Dutch Doctor might not ever want to say hi. 24-me ran out of the apartment, ran to tire himself out, to go back to sleep, to the safer reality that the dream was not dead.

But the stone of *that* fear had been turned. Releasing it, spreading it like an eerie fog within...then out...*everywhere* as 24-me exited the building into the dark bewitching hour of the city. Where the edge of the forest disappeared, and 24-me was alone within it, once again, engulfed in the fear of letting Him go... forever.

***

It was an unusually warm November night. The bars were just closing. The weekenders were still out partying through the night, escaping the day, escaping their lives. Whether it was the stress of the pandemic, the economics of losing jobs or the grief of losing loved ones, it seemed that the city had become a mecca of escape. Every weekend since I'd returned from Amsterdam, visitors seemed to be escaping whatever *their* problems were, intoxicating their minds and bodies on whatever, *beyond* belief. People were drunk, high...*everywhere*. No judgment of course! I get it.

Considering the state I was in, NYC truly had turned into a spooky *sprookje* forest. I wandered toward the Hudson to try to get away from what seemed like goblins of the night. But they were there too, doing drugs, being loud, and giving me moments of fear. I kept walking toward Christopher Street Pier, back to the water, where it was quieter. I was tired. I could not run from the pain of that— potential—reality that a nearly eighteen-year-old dream was dying. The weight of that thought finally broke my heart, and I fell into the frozen waters of it.

He didn't break it.

He didn't do anything.

Which was exactly the catalyst needed that could only come from Him, because my 24-year-old's heart was frozen...only for Him. His silence forced me to go within, to choose myself, to declare it! With that declaration, the curse's cure that had always been within my frozen heart rumbled like a volcano, ready to erupt. It was the first step for me to allow it to break—finally—so that it could break open.

The cure's potion had been slowly melting ever since the letter was sent from the warmth of the gift of love that I gave myself by telling Him. Like a dam that couldn't hold it any longer, cracking a little every day there was no response, and finally bursting that early morning along the Hudson. Allowing the cure to flood throughout my body, filling me with—love, of course—the cure for anything.

The space in my heart I held for twenty-one years for Him to fill—before I understood my first love was me—was now being filled by me. I knew I was on the right road when J. Lo popped on my screen over the holidays and confirmed the love of my life...was me; that every heartbreak—right up to the current one—really was a yellow brick road, leading me home, to myself.

Just as the piece I unconsciously relied on Mike to love unconditionally, before I learned to do it myself, the intimate love I wanted to give to Him, I first had to give to myself by breaking the Catholic Church curse. The curse that told me I couldn't be loved like *that* by a *man*; that I couldn't be loved like *that* by Him or by myself...to be loved, just as I was.

The rushing, cleansing cure spread throughout and went to work, dissolving and transmuting the pain into love. The pain that my ego resisted because it feared not knowing true love without Him. Until the love was absorbed by my ego and washed away the limiting belief that it had to be sought externally in Him, the pain would have to be felt. Then, I could set Him free, and in doing so, set me free.

And *yes!*

It hurt!

Yeah!

I cried!

Like over a year prior, when I broke down near the same pier, over the loss of my friend Mike and the loss of myself. Now it felt like the loss of another friend and the dream of Him. The death of a dream which twenty years and thousands of dollars were invested into. Plus, perhaps I'd say...half a million words written...all for the hope of a few words in return...one sentence...*Hallo, mijn naam is...*(Hello my name is...).

Absolutely, I cried. I cried like a teenager with a broken heart over his first love, along with the fear that I'd never have a love like *that* again. So what if my first love-broken heart got delayed by a couple of decades into middle age and came after my heart broke with Dante? Who said life was linear? If that makes me a freak then just add it to this Misfit Toy's list, a fool, and a freak...here I am.

For anyone that has seen *Boys in the Band,* and more importantly, for any gay man that understands through their own *Boys in the Band* experience, it hurts to have that reality shatter. Bernard displays it pretty well in the film—with all the years of hope *crumbling.*

But *why?*

Why was I crying at the pier—what seemed like—so often? The pier surged in its resurrection as a happy site—briefly—when I saw Him there in the rebirth of spring, creating the possibility to say, "Hey! You've been a muse! Isn't that cool?" I had tried so hard to reestablish the pier with more good memories after my initial breakdown, which had overshaddowed previous ones. And now, with his lack of response, it was a crumbled sore spot again, creating yet another.

So, *yes,* I cried, as one does when something hurts. It relieves the body of countless toxins that contribute to stress. It's healthy. Breakdowns are really breakthroughs required to upgrade to a new version of ourselves. It's not a sign of weakness, no matter what anybody says. It's healing. And above all—Him or no Him—I wanted to heal first, for me, for my second chance.

Fuck, I thought the next day, though.

Scooter.

I had commissioned a painting from Scooter upon returning from Amsterdam. We had discussed it at the beginning of the year—before Him and Christopher Street Pier. I'd seen an artwork of a single orange tulip that I loved. I knew Scooter was great with floral paintings. I made a sketch of some tulips that winter with the colors I wanted as a guide. I did a photo shoot with Elodie *blooming* after her third birthday amongst a bunch of tulips in a garden in April when I visited her for her birthday. Later that month, there were also beautiful orange tulips on the Christopher Street Pier that I photographed.

I've always loved spring in the city for the tulips. The city really does a wonderful job with it. Many thanks to the Netherlands for all the bulbs after 9/11. I probably have thousands of tulip pictures on my phone over the years. So between my sketch, "Tulip Elodie" pictures, and the pier pictures, I was finally ready for Scooter to create something.

But that morning, I regretted the decision for the commission. No offense, Scooter! Or I hoped he at least wouldn't use the pictures from the pier too much in the piece. I didn't need any more reminders of the pier, crying at it, and Him. Scooter, however, went to work on it right away when I asked him in October. And the next afternoon, after the most recent tears at the pier, I received a text from Scooter, a picture. My first look at what he created.

Of course Scooter used the pier pictures mostly, and the result was *stunning*. It took my breath away. I never would have imagined Scooter would create something so colorful and happy and...*gorgeous!* "Getting flowers" from a friend the day after a broken heart—unbeknownst to Scooter—after feeling so sad, began cheering me up. It started to make the pier a happy spot for me again and in that moment, magical.

***

After that day, any part of me that hadn't done so before, consciously or unconsciously, began choosing myself—which was strange. We're taught to think of others first, to put others first. Especially from organized religion, and that it's selfish to choose yourself first. Nope. Not anymore. It's self-*full.*

For over a decade, I heard it *constantly* through the religion of the airlines and safety videos. I said it *myself* when I did the demonstration. Yes, the airlines got it right! Put your own mask on first before helping others! Fill your own cup up first, with love, until it overflows! Then give some of *that* to others. Sure there may be times when yours runs low and doesn't overflow because of what life throws your way, but as fellow human beings that's okay, too. Sometimes, we can help someone refill theirs back up, until they can again themselves.

I wanted to be that person who chooses himself first. Who has healthy boundaries and does what's best for him to maintain alignment and balance in heart, mind, and soul. Then allows someone in from *that* space. The person who has done the shadow work, who understands what his triggers are, who can communicate when he is triggered, and who knows what he needs to work through them. But most importantly, I wanted to be the person that knew there might be setbacks to unconditionally loving himself through life, and to do so without self-judgment or criticism.

Yes, as long as I worked on loving myself like that, I would have the relationship I'd always dreamt of. The manifestation of that, the best version of me, would come in an external 3D human form...or not, and either way, I'd be okay. Because as Gloria taught, there are always moments of love to be experienced...everywhere, all the time.

***

To find the golden thread of poetic justice and pull it through, I would think of Amp and consider what if he did get the Dutch Doctor's information. If my broken heart had to happen because He had rejected Amp's offer to introduce us, I had to find a measure of gratitude for the way it happened.

I thank Amp.

I thank Him.

I thank each for triggering a deep inner wound: for feeling like a fool for doing *all* this and facing the reality of an unrequited—romantic, or now, even platonic—love, and rejection. I mean please, between writing and men combined, I've been rejected probably hundreds of times. But the one rejection my inner 24-me didn't think I could survive was from Him. But I'm here to write the tale, and I'm still alive.

How could I not be grateful to them both for bringing those buried feelings and fears to the surface, to be felt, released, and healed from in order to grow and evolve? Yes, enormous gratitude to Him for being on the street *that* day, at that *exact* moment, and gratitude to Amp for thinking to introduce us. They both played a part that set my healing journey in motion over the previous two years.

I can't know for sure, but I'm fairly certain, knowing what the broken heart with Mike felt like, and the one with Him, I don't think my heart could have taken the loss of two friends in 2020, imaginary or not. It definitely would have been much more difficult in the space I was in that year...that, I am certain. Yes, if Amp did make a decision to be the guardian of my feelings after seeing how excited I was because I had been rejected right from the beginning, then I'm grateful that his actions did delay it.

Perhaps the pain needed to be spaced out. Perhaps I never would have been inspired to write the play had I turned around or had Amp introduced us. It has always been for my healing first and foremost. Whether in dreams or sightings, the inspiration continued to reflect to me, through this one man, what I needed to heal in myself. Again why Him? Ask science if they can prove a reason yet.

In addition to all the learning about PTSD and trauma that was created by not turning around or being introduced, perhaps there is a bonus: that it can help others to relate to their own experiences. Whomevers eyes' *this* lands upon.

Sure I felt a bit melancholy for what seemed like the loss of my muse too. I couldn't see how the story, the *working* relationship with Him could continue from *here*. No, this writing...right *here*...would *have* to be the last of the entire twenty-five-year journey of wanting to write *one* book.

Wow, nearly twenty years from the first writing of Him, and not even a "hello"—talk about The Fool-feeling being amplified. I get it. The irony is not lost on me.

But maybe!

One day, people will think it *is* a myth or an urban legend about...The Fool.

"Hey, Bob! You hear about that guy that didn't even ask his first love's name and then spent like twenty years searching and writing like half a dozen books about Him, so he *could* meet Him and learn His name. But when he *did* find Him, it was through a letter that he made contact, and he not only didn't get the guy's name, he didn't even get a hello! Can you believe it? Ha! What a fool!"

"Nahhhh Fred, that didn't *really* happen! That's one of those urban legends."

"No! I swear! I know a guy, who knows a girl, who knows a cousin of his."

"Excuse me, Bob," I'd proudly say after overhearing their conversation at the next table. "But Fred is right...that *actually* happened and I! I am *that* Fool!"

***

The following week I hopped on a train to Stonington Borough. I ran to Dante with my broken heart. With this one, it felt as if I was drowning. The shock of the thought that the tiniest aspect of this dream would not come true felt suffocating; my ego was gasping for air.

When Dante picked me up at the train station, I was dying to tell someone about the letter, about the no response. I had not told anyone about the letter except my therapist and Mila. I knew that of all people, Dante would be able to empathize how heartbreaking it would be to me. Knowing how long of a journey it had been. He was the one who originally encouraged me to continue the writing. Yes, he would understand. Still, I didn't know how to bring it up. I waited until we got back to the borough.

Dante had been on the phone, texting and talking with his sister, Shirley, in Florida for most of the time we drove to his home. I was sitting at the kitchen table waiting for him to get off another phone call so we could go for some nature in the borough, be by the ocean, to calm and soothe my anxiety. Yes, I would tell him then, with the fresh air and the immense support of the ocean behind me. But then I overheard him suggest to Shirley that they call in a priest, and that he would look into flights to Florida. I knew what that meant.

Mother Mary—like the head of a convent, as Shirley and Dante liked to refer to her because of her strong commitment to the old school Catholic Church, a woman who *only* watched the Catholic channel, (I didn't even know there was a Catholic channel)—was dying. I'd heard about Mother Mary for a few years before I even met her, as she and Dante had been estranged at the time. Sometimes her commitment to Catholicism clashed with having a gay son. But when Dante and Mother Mary were talking again, and I was invited to her home for a traditional Portuguese meal, I quietly chuckled when I walked into her apartment, and sure enough, the Catholic channel was on!

Mother Mary had been basically dying from *something* for six years. Yet she held on through it all—with tenacious Portuguese explorer blood and strength packed into her petit 5'1" stature—until now. She was getting ready to make her exploration...to the other side.

"You can stay if you want for a couple days. But I have to go to Florida tomorrow," Dante said after he got off the phone and began looking for plane tickets.

"Yes, of course. I'm so sorry," I said. "Are you okay?"

"I just feel numb. This has been a long time coming. Shirley and I are both numb."

"Let's go for a walk in the borough and get some nature."

Dante had been living where he grew up, a stone's throw away from his grandparents', aunts', and uncles' former homes. We walked toward Wall Street to wander Dodge Paddock and Beal Preserve, a nature spot tucked away—if you don't know the locale—with a small field right on the edge of the ocean. It was a favorite spot of Dante's as a kid. He pointed out all the former houses of his family members, relaying old memories as we literally walked down his memory lane.

He seemed in as good a place as possible for the circumstances. He and his sister had been committed for years to the care of their mother. I had watched it make him stronger, more resilient. They both soldiered on with each health complication or need for Mother Mary. They knew this day was coming and that there would be a release of peace for their mother and for them, while they took into account the moment that it was the death of their mother. Dante and Mother Mary had a long, complicated history. Yet the love was there, and the time to say good-bye had come.

We took in the ocean, walking the rocks once we got there. I walked out on the long line of boulders that stretched into the ocean, while Dante stayed by the shore. I looked out to the sea. As the moment presented itself to tell Dante, it felt strange; to talk to my ex about my first love, whom had no idea He *was* my first love, who for 99% of the relationship was a muse who was now, I was 99% sure, a doctor in my neighborhood and an actual 3D person, who now knew that I had dreamt of meeting Him, and there had been no response, and my heart was broken and, and, and...I think that's the gist. Yeah, it felt a bit strange and confusing and t felt The Fool again. But the ocean helped calm my spirit.

I turned around, walked back to the shore, and told Dante about Him as the tears choked me. Hearing it aloud, out in the world, and not in my therapist's office to be analyzed, made it more real. Ever the soldier of love, Dante's comfort was received and welcomed. I began to wonder how we had been pulled together in this moment, our hearts both breaking, to be there for one another, like old times.

My head was conscious of the high emotions, whether this was a door to reenter or if our hearts simply needed a friend. We went to bed around midnight after a nice dinner at the Ocean House in Westerly. We both deserved a special evening out and the chance to celebrate Mother Mary. It wasn't but an hour later that the phone started ringing. There was no response from Mother Mary, and Shirley was on her way to the retirement community to confirm, then relay the news, after another hour had passed, that she was dead.

My thoughts went to how beautifully karmic it was that I could be there for Dante in the middle of the night with such news that a parent had died. Just as he had been there for me when we were together, and I had received the call in the middle of the night that my father had died. After phone calls back and forth to everyone, until about four in the morning, we finally fell asleep.

Two hours later, my mind succumbed. It could no longer escape the new reality—He was not going to call. It could no longer resist the last bit of air squeezing out of the dream. It could no longer resist drowning in love's potion and receiving the love saved for Him for so long. I immediately sat up in bed and gasped for a breath, as if I was born into a new life, surrendering to the dream's death to start a new day and begin walking the road of acceptance.

Dante decided there was no need for him to travel to Florida. He would rather stay in Connecticut to meet with the funeral director while his brother made the trip to help Shirley prepare to bring Mother Mary home. I was glad I would not be left alone after all.

Dante and I were both zombies in our surreal new worlds. It helped to escape into his world, to try to forget about the city and Him. Useless. The fragility in the air was palpable. I felt on the verge of tears all day long, but wanted to remain strong for Dante and whatever he might need.

Whenever I'm blue, a piece of sage advice stored in me bubbles up. It is from Neal, one of my regular's from The Klatch in Laguna Beach. Neal ran the porno shack in Laguna, across from The Boom Boom Room, and gave me free porn. Back when rentals were not on DVD…but VHS! Thanks Neal!

"When you're blue, help someone else," he said to me one day, sensing I was sad. So I tried to help Dante.

***

While Dante ran errands, I walked to the point in the borough to sit on du Bois Beach and have a moment with Mother Mary, say my peace, and wish her Godspeed. The anger I always felt toward the Church for the mental and emotional abuse of my young mind and heart was triggered.

I hated the Catholic Church at that moment. I hated everything about it. My heart and mind felt like Jenny from Forest Gump. When she returned to her father's house as an adult, with rage she picked up every stone she could find to hurl at his house, for the abuse she received from her father. I wanted to throw the boulders that stretched into the ocean ahead of me at the Catholic Church, a boulder for every possible one. While the adult in me tried to soothe and convince my triggered inner child to let go.

I returned my thoughts to Mother Mary and the conservativeness of the old-school Catholic Church she represented so well. I was always a bit on edge in her presence, on my best behavior—the conservative handshakes she gave, her reserved energy in my presence—her son's homosexual lover.

I hated the Catholic Church for that too, that I couldn't have a "typical" relationship with a "mother-in-law." The conditioned beliefs in her created what felt like a boundary between us, and kept me from feeling like I had a second mother in her. Although, Dante and his mother did have many positive experiences as well that Dante would mention, ever the peacemaker and forgiver that he is. But, when the conditioned beliefs took over, well, it seemed unnecessary for him and unfair for us.

I knew Mother Mary had many wonderful qualities and was deeply loved by Dante. I had heard of another side of her that was fun and light. I really wanted my "talk" with her at du Bois—my own personal good-bye—to be peaceful and genuine.

I thought of the one memory I did have that showed her playful side. She was in a good space after Dante and I arrived in Florida and reunited with her, Shirley, and the nieces during a visit. I was expecting my usual handshake greeting. Mother Mary did extend her hand but then pulled me in and gave a kiss on each cheek. I was floored, and delighted.

When we ate dinner that night, Mother Mary sat next to *me!* The giggly-girl side that I had always heard of bubbled out. She was having *fun*, and let loose with a little wine. She expressed such *joyous* laughter as she shared embarrassing stories about Dante in her classic high-pitched, Portuguese accented voice— which Dante could impersonate *perfectly,* and always made me laugh when he did. I felt I had a moment of love—like with Gloria—and acceptance with Mother Mary that night. For that moment—and for making Dante—I wished her well at our private memorial at du Bois.

I thought of some of the people *in* the Catholic Church who I have been exposed to over the years. I could appreciate the many honorable people that it did contain. The positive work for humanity those *individuals* did. I separated them from the institution that created so much pain for so many LGBTQIA human beings over the years with their abusive dogma.

I rose from the sand, walked to the line of boulders that I wanted to drop on every church, stepped on top, and walked out to the last one. Then thanked the Church for the lessons they reflected to me. Pushing me to dig deeply to love myself in the areas they told me I couldn't, that were ugly. I thanked them for making me stronger for it, and then forgave them. Finally. Forgiveness was the key, the final blow to its foundational hold on me.

One of the original dreams of Gloria from many years ago came back to me. My family and I were visiting her at an estate. When we arrived, Gloria excitedly whisked me up the grand staircase to share something with me while my family waited downstairs. Afterward we all went underneath the mansion, where the dream became strange.

The home was built on Catholic catacombs. We were there for the funeral of my father's father. There were priests leading the way, pallbearers carrying a casket, as my family and Gloria followed behind. We climbed mounds of dirt up into gradually tinier spaces, the darkness illuminated only by candles. Bricks were falling down. I remember how claustrophobic and unsafe it felt as the foundation was clearly crumbling.

Perhaps it was a symbolic premonition dream for years later on du Bois Beach, foretelling the death to the ancient patriarchal hierarchy system, which does not work anymore. It was the Church's tower moment to fall, once and for all. Giving It a chance to rebuild with more kindness. While setting me free from it, as free as the open ocean before me.

***

I felt like Philomena, Judi Dench's character in *Philomena*. After her long, emotionally arduous search—which I could relate to—for her son, who was taken from her by the convent as a child because she was "bad" for having premarital sex. The longing Philomena had for *years* to find him—which I could also relate to—never knowing the evil head nun of the convent purposely prevented her from *ever* finding him. Until Philomena is standing at her son's grave—full circle—back at the convent—that part I hoped wasn't true for Him.

Oh, Judi! You are amazing! Your acting! Incredible! I could feel *all* of the heartache, of *all* those years of hope, only to find out, that her son was *dead*. On top of that, what the nun had done in preventing the reunion. Just *one* example of the Church's evil over the years, as it is a true story. Empathizing, when I first saw it, brought tears to my eyes.

But the surprise was the next part of the scene. *The* moment of the film that exemplified the humanity we all could learn from. Facing the evil nun after realizing what she had done, looking at her, saying to her, "I forgive you."

"*What,* just like that?" the reporter who helped Philomena on the search for her son, asks.

"Not just like that," Philomena replies. "That's hard. That's hard for me. But I don't want to hate people," her wisdom replies.

I felt like that.

No, not just like that, was I able to forgive the Catholic Church. It took most of my adult life to comprehend, and rectify the damage through self-love. And like Philomena—that was *really* hard. But it wasn't doing me any good not to forgive, not to let go, and move onward.

198

Now...knock it off! I added to my thoughts of forgiveness to the Church, carried in the air out to the ocean. Just as my father used to say to me and my brothers when we were being naughty.

Afterward, I walked down Water Street through the borough back to Dante's place. When I crossed Wadawanuck Square and passed the library, St. Mary's Church came into view. Mother Mary would be making her way there for her last good-bye in a week. The scene, the colors of the sky with the clouds behind the steeple as the dusk of a New England autumn approached, was *beautiful*. I could see the beauty in all of it.

I wanted to remain strong for Dante, who appeared stronger than I, whether numb, at peace, or both, with Mary's passing, while I felt like a mess. I tried to keep it together, tried to respect Dante's loss. It felt more of a priority than my "loss" of a muse and a friend. It seemed secondary.

I accompanied Dante to the funeral home in Mystic to speak with the director and confirm the plans they had made years before when Mary's death "began." The director pulled out the binder of caskets to make sure they were in agreement with what was chosen. When I saw the casket and what it was called my eyes watered. Mary was to be buried in the Orchid casket. She was born on Madeira Island where orchids grow wild and free all over. Orchids, again, and now associated with a casket? Are you kidding me? Was this really happening? Was this decades-long dream *really* dead and being buried in an orchid casket?

Thank goodness the tension broke with tearful laughter moments later. I was delightfully surprised to learn about another side of Mother Mary. Dante made a request to the funeral director that a piece of fern be placed in the casket with his mother...between her legs.

"What?!" I exclaimed. "You want to put a *fern* between your mother's legs?"

Dante laughed out loud. Which made me laugh out loud, which we both *desperately* needed.

"It was Shirley's idea," Dante began to explain through laughter.

Of course, it was Shirley's idea, I thought.

Mother Mary had a love of plants. She also had the gift of caring for them. Plants thrived vibrantly with life all over Dante's childhood home. It is one of his fondest memories of his mother and their family home.

Decades' prior, when she immigrated to America from Madeira, Mother Mary wanted to bring a piece of her birthplace to her adopted country. She took a section of a fern and hid it between her legs for the plane ride. She thought she might get in trouble for bringing a plant from another ecosystem into a new one. She was successful! The plant had produced many babies for decades, and Shirley still had the original one.

Oh, Mother Mary! I love you even more. Not so innocent and pious after all! Smuggling plants into a foreign country! You got away with it! Fabulous! Great idea, Shirley!

We headed to Mystic Pizza for a slice. I wanted to burst out crying, but cared to respect Dante's situation more. I wondered if we were being pulled together again, perhaps for a second chance through loss. My head, aware that emotions were running high and all over the place, logically thought, *perhaps my heart is reaching. Maybe this wasn't the best space to approach the idea of a rekindled romance, to fill a void created by loss,* my head cautioned my heart. I couldn't take it any longer, all of the emotion from Him, the Church, sadness for Dante, Shirley, and of course for Mother Mary. I had to let the tears out for it all. And I did, all over my Mystic Pizza.

I couldn't believe how *fragile* I felt, like I was losing another long time best friend. That night I walked out alone through the quiet borough toward the beach at Diving Street, lit by the approaching shining, full moon.

"I have to let go, I have to let go, I have to let go," I repeated while pacing in the sand. It was as if the rippled vibrations of the words needed to travel down to the core of *that* fear, as deep as the Mariana Trench, to trigger what most needed to be healed, once and for all. The only one that could trigger it was Him. The only one that could heal it was I. By loving myself in that place—like with Mike—where the 24-me had reserved space for Him alone to love me.

Rejection is a way to teach the rejected they can live without the other. Yes, I knew I could live without Him. I had done so for many years and had many wonderful life experiences and relationships. The unconscious fear—that I would never accomplish the dream to at least meet Him again—was perhaps what my inner child thought I could not live without. Now, I was consciously facing that fear. But I had to revert back to the fact that the most important part of the dream was accomplished, the dying regret was rectified...He knew.

"It's the heart, afraid of breaking, that never learns to dance," Bette sang. I *was* afraid of a broken heart over Him, and it did feel like I wouldn't learn to dance again—metaphorically speaking through life...of course! I mean, *come on!*

I learned in the clubs of London and in clubs around the world, picking up moves by watching and mimicking some of the best dancers. I know how to dance, *that* I'm confident about!

"*It's the dream afraid of waking that never takes the chance,*" Bette continues. I was afraid of waking from the dream, yet, I had taken the chance. Now, it seemed I had awoken to the dream drifting away, like the Heart of the Ocean diamond in the waters that stretched before me. But, like Rose and Jack, now you all know that there once was a man, who I met in the dark.

It felt lonely, and a bit lost, like an adventurer who holds fast to a singular life-long quest, to discover that his mission could no longer be. Who *was* I without this story, without the co-creator of it? What would I do now that this series was apparently finished with the unexpected surprise ending/beginning of *something* else? Oh, I felt lonely. There was no one I could turn to that knew *this* particular experience. Who meets someone for a romantic time, runs, doesn't get His name, searches and writes about Him for years, longing and hoping to meet again, only to give a letter to Him twenty years later, which bore no response? Nobody in the history of the human race. There was nobody I could turn to who could say, "I know what it's like. It will be okay." *No one*...except me.

Just like there was nobody on the face of the planet, or in the history of the human race that would have His experience—which He had no idea He *even* had—of being my muse in this way. It was looking like, He never would know.

It was an isolating experience to work through or even describe. The closest depiction I could use for this one-of-a-kind feeling is again by using art—it's *so* important—with the medium of film combining *Ladies in Lavender* and *Life of Pi*. Dame Judi and your brilliant acting! I felt like *both* she and Dame Maggie in the film, *Ladies in Lavender.* When the Polish boy that washed up on shore, whom they took in and cared for—and whom Judi's character falls in love with—leaves one day without a goodbye. Judi's reaction to his departure reveals that she is a middle-aged woman with the emotional maturity of a young lady, who had never experienced falling in love, or a broken heart. Ohhhh, Dame Dench—such an amazing scene. One could see in your eyes when the character's heart breaks, the moment she realizes it is an unrequited love.

As Dame Smith's character looks on, she is *completely* surprised at the breakdown of tears her sister displays. Before realizing it is her sister's first broken heart. The tenderness and love she then gives to her sister are beautiful.

Dench was 24-me and Smith was 45-me. My heart broke for Him, as it faced the fear that was also deep within for two decades, that *if ever* the third-dimensional boy—now a man—was found, that it would also be unrequited.

I cried at what seemed like a break-up with my muse. *All* that time we spent "together" over the years was like the end of the film, *Life of Pi* when they reach the shore and Richard Parker gets off the boat and walks away without a second look; no acknowledgment for what they shared. Nothing. Pi is shocked. One interpretation of the film is that Richard Parker did not really exist and was a reflection of all the parts of himself that Pi needed to look at. Not that He—the 3D He—owed me anything, or didn't exist. Yet He reflected all the parts within that were the roadblocks on my journey home to self-love that needed to be seen, addressed, validated, and loved. It also meant opening my heart, bringing the love out of me that was already there.

***

The night I returned to the city, Dante took me to his studio at The Velvet Mill. He held some art of mine that I wanted, in order to continue redecorating. It had been an emotional few days, going through them together, being there for one another like when we were a couple. Yes, my tender heart still wondered if perhaps we were being led back to each other.

We were talking about the play in the car. Dante was still the most intimate and consistent confidant and sounding board I'd had for my writing for many years. As always, he, versus my resistance, was supporting and encouraging of it.

"I absolutely can *not* put it out now."

"Why not? Maybe it helps other people," he said.

I'd feel like a fool, life can be so cruel, don't know what to doooooo, Celine's words came back to my mind.

"Because! Ohhh, I don't know! It hurts! I can't believe after all these years, three books, a play, a song, a search, and I don't even get to say 'hi' or learn His name? He doesn't even want to say 'hi' to me...once? I just can't believe it!"

"Maybe you and your readers aren't supposed to know His name."

"Don't say that!" I snapped back. My tender heart was still not ready to let go of even that small aspect of the dream of Him.

When we entered his studio Dante had mood lights already on for ambience, and played some relaxing music. My heart began to beat a little faster and wondered...*should* it be open to the possibility of Dante and Anthony 2.0? I was walking around admiring Dante's latest pieces, while Dante went through his drawers looking for my art.

"Hey! Look what I found!" Dante excitedly said after a couple minutes.

I assumed it was the piece I wanted and turned around, only to see layed out on his table, not the art piece I was looking for...but a poster. My heart stopped. I wanted to cry. *He* had been out of my mind for many moments. Then made a return. Lying on the table was an old poster for the launch of the original *Amsterdam Angel* with the nearly nine-year-old 12-12-12 date underneath it staring back at me in the face.

John Cusack and *Serendipity* returned to my thoughts. When his fiancé gives him a book after their wedding rehearsal, he opens it to find out it's *the* book with *Her*—the person who for years *he's* been looking for—number in it.

Ring, ring, hello?

I felt like that, only with one *big* difference. He—supposedly—already had my number. But for whatever—valid—reason was choosing not to use it. Yet I took it as my *Alchemist* omen delivered through Dante. The professional aspect of Him as The Muse and this story was telling me to move forward with it.

All right, I'll put it out, I thought to whomever was guiding me...a god, a gut, a muse. Perhaps all three were one in the same.

***

On the way to the train station in Westerly, we drove by an enormous rock on the lawn of an apartment complex that had something spray-painted in white on it.

"Stop the car! Go back, please!" I said. "I want to see what's painted on that rock."

Dante turned around and pulled off to the side of the road when we approached. I couldn't tell in the dark what was on the rock. I got out of the car for a closer look. A feeling of peace blanketed me. I was both surprised, and not surprised when I read the words on it, understanding at this point my friendship with magic. How it pops in—often when needed—like a friend, the external reflecting the internal.

The rock: a reminder of the note card that I had placed on my bulletin board after returning from Amsterdam weeks earlier. The intention I had set to build my second chance at life from a strong foundation of peace and love. It was *plenty* to rebuild from. The rock a manifestation of it with the spray-painted words:

Peace

Love

***

For my readers who have followed this journey with me since *Amsterdam Angel* came out nearly ten years ago and who may have been curious or wondered, like me, what His actual name is, I can't tell you as I write this, or perhaps ever. But I can think of no better name in the interim than Michael.

Yes, Michael, for my lost innocence, for the mirror soul who helped me to grow, and in honor of Mike, who set this odyssey in motion, and was the catalyst for two stars colliding in the dark, once upon a bewitching December night, in a little village called Amsterdam. And for a surname, well, why not the sign that led me to Him: Dutchman Contractors—sans Contractors.

Yes, Michael Dutchman, that seems appropriate. Doctor, that is.

There is a name for you, for me, for my first love and muse.

He is not an angel, not a hallucination, but an actual human being.

Dr. Michael Dutchman, my innocence—lost in Amsterdam and found again in New Amsterdam. Forever lost and found, an eternal dance of peek-a-boo pop-ins in dreams, sightings, and inspiration.

If, in this incarnation, I never find out His name, perhaps one day, Gloria's words will ring true. She'll appear in a dream showing me her latest dress, one beautiful bird-chirping afternoon, or she'll be waiting to greet me and take me dress shopping with her when I get to the other side—again—and as I zip her up, I can say, "Gloria, you were right. Knowing His name…it seemed important at the time."

What's in a name anyway? Whatever that Shakespeare guy said about roses. It still smells the same whatever you call it. Whether the love is given the name, **This**—as He stated—**Is**—still—**Love**. Gloria didn't get my name, I didn't get hers, but it didn't prevent our moment of love.

At the same time, I will continue to embrace Gloria's *other* sentiment that *anything* is possible. The phone could ring one day, and life can change in an instant. Or *someone* could be walking down the street one day—and change my life...again.

Someone said, "All it takes is a single person, a single moment to change the tide of life." For me, there have been four such people that have changed the tide of my life. Some more than once, and one I've never even met: Mike, Him, Amp, and whoever the human resources person is at the hospital who made the final decision to hire Him, and bring Him to my neighborhood. Whoever *you* are...big kiss to you.

Regardless, the hospital got a donation for that move. My "bill" for the most inadvertent assistance from one of their newest doctors. He was first on the scene as I woke into a second life. He made a house call twice—and a pier-call—to check on my progress. Of course, the hospital doesn't have any record of the services He provided, or even knows about it...until now.

And before I cross over permanently, it's not about giving up or not giving up on a dream, moving on or not moving on, but rather, loving...and letting go of the muse, who supposedly is a doctor.

Yes, I have wished, at times, that I had someone I could have turned to for help or guidance throughout this incarnation. But whether I wanted to recognize, listen to, trust in, or believe in Him, I have always had someone. He's always been there. He will always be there. Just as I've always been, and will always be, there for Him. I surrender to that. The promise I made long ago in a pink birdhouse.

But a three-dimensional person still would have been nice to help with the isolating aspects of this experience because it goes beyond that of a writer writing. It's like trying to convince and share with the world that you have this really *amazing* imaginary friend...except, He's *real.* Yes, if only there was someone who was around that could relate to that, it would be incredibly advantageous.

Oh wait!

There *is* someone that can relate! Albeit, he is not of the human species but the bird variety. Big Bird! Where are you Big Bird? I need your help! Can somebody tell me how to get...how to get to Sesame Street? Big Bird can relate with his friend, Aloysius—Mr. Snuffleupagus that is. For many years, Big Bird tried to convince the people in *his* neighborhood Aloysius was real. *They* all thought he was an imaginary friend, too, until, one day, Big Bird was able to reveal Mr. Snuffleupagus to the world.

Just call me Big Bird and Him. Well, maybe *I* will call him Snuffy, as a term of endearment for Dr. Michael Dutchman, until I can reveal Him to the people in my Chelsea neighborhood.

***

But really?

HRH The Prince of Sprookje, Dr. Michael Dutchman, Mooie Man van de Donkere, Amsterdam Angel, Snuffy, Meneer Muze…really? You don't want to say "hi" just once? I get it! It hurt! If the only reason you'd accept for me walking by again was that I better be coming back from the dead…then I was! I was coming back from the dead!

You're the one that proposed the hypothesis that "This is Love." Perhaps magic and miracles are not in scientists'—or doctors'—vocabulary. But it is just unproven science. So this is my logical explanation of your proposed hypothesis through my own scientific method. Showing you all the reasons through all the people through all the years—with documented magical proof—why, you were right. Maybe it might surprise even Yourself how right you were.

Doc, come on, could I at least write You a check for the time You put in as The Muse? For asking and answering the all-important question that started it all? Well…for that…I need your name!

***

One name you're not getting from *me*, for sure, is my therapist's. As you can see, she's good. I'm not risking all her spots filling up and me getting knocked out of line. Let's just call her my Mrs. Potts, who helped this Beast find his Beauty within, by reflecting it on my street, at my doorstep, at the pier, and within many dreams, meditations, sightings, and ketamine sessions, with these never-ending magical moments.

Of course, there *is* the chance that He is not *the* Dutch Doctor/Amsterdam Angel that I attribute to being one and the same. I believe scientists don't like to use 100% in saying one thing or another. I think the number used when they're *pretty* certain is 99.7%. So I, too, will adopt that measure of certainty that it is Him.

But, in the 0.3% chance he's not, then I suppose I would be The Fool. And whomever the Dutch Doctor is that got flowers…twice…and a really long letter, *he* may *still* be scratching his head. I hope he at least enjoyed the flowers.

Even if proved not wrong, I'll still proudly take on the title of The Fool! You were right, Mr. Thackeray, "love make fools of us all." Would *you* want it any other way? At this point, I'm not sure I would. Life might not be as entertaining to live—or read about—in my humble opinion, if we didn't have a little fool-for-love in us.

Besides, in the tarot deck, The Fool is standing on the edge of a cliff, about to skip off the precipice into the unknown, with no worries because he's willing to take the leap of faith to start his expedition and trust that somehow he will *not* fall. And when it comes to love, The Fool means optimism and fun. He easily attracts love. In fact The Fool loves love just as much as he loves his freedom. Which is the best way to love—unconditionally—someone...me...you...Him.

So in that perspective of The Fool, then Yes!

I am!

Ab! So! Lute! Ly!

The Fooooooool!

A fool for fairy tales.

Because as Frank sang, "Fairy tales can come true, it can happen to you...to me...if you're young at heart!"

So until then, I *will* keep my heart young and open to *anything*, and *everyone*. Even dear reader...to **you**!

***

Have there been any more dreams as of this writing?

Yes.

One was hot, *hot* sex. That was a first, in the dream world anyway—it was nearly twenty-one years since we had sex. Maybe it was break-up sex with my muse. Maybe it was make-up up sex with my muse; as it was right around the time I really dove into the creative surge to write *this* piece. Just when I didn't think He could inspire anymore, I was proved wrong.

A week later I dreamt that I was at someone's house for a dinner party. The doorbell rang. I offered to get the door for the host. When I opened it, there He was. We looked at each other, both a bit surprised, but smiling, as neither one of us could run at that point. For some reason, Mr. Rogers's style, I offered to take his coat and replace it with a hoodie for dinner. I offered Him a green hoodie—which

I was wearing *that* day—or a red one. He chose red. We sat at the table smiling like, okay, finally...hello.

That was followed by a dream where I was looking at an apartment to rent above a restaurant when the owner said "I have a surprise for you!" Then a fancy SUV limo drove into the apartment and He popped out looking like a rock star. We hugged and I apologized for walking by. It was a happen reunion, but too quick of a visit. He had to run, to a concert, or something. I don't know.

"Wait, wait," I said. "I never got your name."

Just as He was telling me His name, a *marching band* appeared on both sides of us and started playing celebratory music, while He continued talking.

"Den," He continued.

"What? Wait! I didn't catch that. What was your name?" I asked again as the band continued to play. "Did you say, Dan?"

"I have family in Den Haag," He carried on sharing about Himself because He didn't hear *me* say that I didn't hear *Him* over the music.

"Wait, you said your name is Dan? Or you have family in Den Haag?" I tried to clarify before He realized His rock star car was waiting.

"I have to run!" Then He gave me a big hug before He got in His car.

Oh, come on Universe! Now you're just taking the piss—as the British say—with me! A marching band? Really? *Right* as I'm doing my *Boys in the Band* confession...in *person*? *Right* as He's telling me His name?

I can't make this stuff up.

Hey Doc! Have You got family in Den Haag? That's what You told me in a dream!

***

The following week I was having lunch in The Rambles after a ketamine session. A mother and daughter were photographing cardinals. I overheard them speaking Dutch.

"*Ben jij Nederlands?*" I asked without flinching, the beginning line of my own play, as life imitated art.

They were from, yup, Den Haag. Coincidence? At this point, I don't believe in them. It wasn't until later that I thought to ask if they knew a Dutch Doctor in New York.

Hey Doc! You got a mom and a sister?

And, yes, He has visited in a few meditations as well.

Explain away, psychologists. Explain that, New Age people. Does it truly matter who is "right"? Neither the mind-based people nor the heart-based people can *truly* prove one way or the other why He has been chosen by life to come to me in this way. If there is, please introduce yourself! I'd really like to meet you!

Until then, it may remain one of—my—life's mysteries. A conversation between individuals use labels based on their life experiences, beliefs, and gut feelings for events that *did* happen, and with the people they happened with. However, I revert to another golden nugget from my therapist, "I hate labels!"

Absolutely!

Who cares?

Who cares?

Who cares who has the "right" or "wrong" label?

None of the labels change the events and dreams that occurred. I have no reason to lie. This is the truth, believe it or not. Perhaps it is hard to believe. If I had not lived it, written it down, and seen it in black and white, I may have trouble believing it, as well.

I wish I were *that* creative. But I'm simply more of a reporter, reporting the events. Ironically, Journalism was the first major I started studying twenty-some years ago at Michigan State.

Even if none of the sightings were Him, there once was a man, a beautiful man in the dark whose outward beauty I did not see initially. Rather, I felt first His inner beauty a long time ago, in a club called Cockring. He *does* exist, and he started it all by proposing one question and one answer that led me on my journey home.

Aren't we all going to the same place anyway? Aren't all the roads we take *leading* to the same place?

Home.

Within.

Aren't we all just helping guide each other home? To "see one another through," as my other muse, and angel, Gloria stated.

Yes! There have been dreams of Gloria, too, as of recently!

I kid you not!

Showing up like any good girlfriend does to hang out. Especially when it is needed to take the mind off men...or muses.

For twenty-one years His energy, in some form, has popped in and it doesn't seem to be going anywhere from the ethers. We'll see if He does when this final piece is complete. Now, I really can't imagine what more there is to write about Him...although, I've been wrong before.

But at least now, He knows...*het was heel speciale voor mij ook*. Why was it important enough for a twenty-one-year search, books, a play, a song, and thousands of dollars later for Him to know?

It just was.

***

Ahhhhh Beautiful Man from the Dark! Why didn't you say, "Michael! Is that *you*?" on that miracle 16th of September afternoon?

I would have said, "Nooooo! Actually, it's *not* Michael! But! It is the *mij* you're thinking of! *Grrreat* to see you! You have *no* idea how great!

> *I believe in miracles*
> *Where you from?*
> *You sexy thing!...*
> *Where did you come from Angel?*
> *How did you know I needed you?...*

What are you doing in my neighborhood?! On my street! I have been thinking about you! I was *just writing* about you! Allow me to buy you a cup of coffee, and I'll explain. I'll tell you a story, a *wild adventure* with a muse I know! There's a great café that has the *best* coffee and gelato in the city just around the corner that I *love* called Lollino's. Let's go!"

RO3235

Made in United States
North Haven, CT
15 March 2023